Praise for Manny Mill
and *Radical Redemption*

I've been part of the Koinonia House Ministry family for over sixteen years. Koinonia House Ministry met me at the gate upon being released from prison November 8, 1996. Without Manny Mill (my spiritual mentor) and the ministry of Koinonia House, I would not have become the man I am today.

—EDDIE WELLS, former resident of the Koinonia
  House Ministry

Manny's enthusiasm for Jesus and his love for the unloved of our society are contagious. His life story demonstrates with dramatic miracles of redemption that in the words of Manny himself, Jesus is the Real Deal!

—HANS FINZEL, bestselling author

Manny Mill is the "real deal"—living proof of the transforming grace of Jesus Christ. Thousands in and out of prison have been challenged by Manny to trust in the radical redeeming power of the Savior. This book will encourage any reader to likewise live with that same purpose and passion.

—HUTZ H. HERTZBERG, executive director,
  The Orchard Network

If there is a question about God's power to radically change a person's life, this is the book to read. It is wonderful to see how God has taken Manny's drive and enthusiasm and focused it on kingdom work.

—JERRY K. ROSE, president, Total Living Network

A blatant reminder that we can't do anything without God—but that with God and through His grace, all things are possible.
—**KEVIN PALAU**, president, Luis Palau Association

Warning: This story is real. And Manny is contagious. Its lesson will more than touch you: it will challenge you to put "shoe leather" to your faith in service to our King.
—**CHUCK MISSLER**, PhD, executive director, Koinonia House Publishers

Anyone who encounters Manny Mill sees "Exhibit A" of God's overpowering love for the lost.
—**HON. PETER J. ROSKAM**, U.S. Representative, 6th Congressional District, IL

Manny Mill is one of those rare people whose story and whose continued faith-filled exuberance lifts all who know him.
—**JOEL NEDERHOOD**, director emeritus of ministries, *The Back to God Hour*; pastor, Cottage Grove Christian Reformed Church, South Holland, IL

Manny Mill is a true trophy of God's grace. His story will gladden your heart.
—**THOMAS C. PRATT**, advisory life director, Prison Fellowship

I am glad to commend the book *Radical Redemption* to all who need to be reminded of the incredible power of the gospel to change a life. God doesn't tweak us a bit; He transforms us. Manny is a living example.
—**LONNIE J. ALLISON**, executive director, Billy Graham Center, Wheaton College

In *Radical Redemption* we read about a man who is running headlong in one direction, meets Christ, reverses course, and runs with new speed for a new purpose. The passion, enthusiasm, and energy that serve hell one minute are serving heaven the next. The honest story of a passionate man gives us all hope that our past need not determine our future.

 —STEPHEN B. KELLOUGH, chaplain,
  Wheaton College

Most of us have come to faith through what would be considered "normal" life circumstances, so it is interesting and exciting to learn how God also sometimes uses the most dramatic and unusual experiences through which to demonstrate His life-changing, transforming power. A compelling read!

 —GUNTHER H. (BUD) KNOEDLER, retired bank
  executive, Chicago

This is a great story of how much God can do with one redeemed sinner who is sold out for Jesus.

 —GAY REYNOLDS, vice president, Quantum
  Professional Search

Radical Redemption is the story of a simple man with an unbelievable passion and love for Jesus. It is a story of one man's journey of falling in love and being "real" for Jesus.

 —JORGE L. VALDES, PhD, national speaker and
  author of *Coming Clean*

Manny Mill is truly a redeemed man! He has moved from a life of corruption and self-interest to one of service and sacrifice. This is a textbook example of how Jesus changes men!

 —MARK ELFSTRAND, morning host, WMBI,
  Chicago

Manny is one of the most persuasive persons I know, and this book sheds light on why I'm now involved in postprison ministry.

—BOB COOK, ministry volunteer

Reading Manny's colorful story is the next best thing to knowing Manny himself and the joyful work God is doing through him among ex-offenders.

—TIMOTHY R. BOTTS, calligraphic artist, senior art director, Tyndale House

Revolutionary! The beauty of Manny's ministry reflects the gospel perfectly. Profoundly simple.

—BISHOP EDWARD PEECHER, pastor, Chicago Embassy Church, Chicago

This book will inspire as well as challenge those who pursue truth and believe God is still able to change lives.

—SAMUEL M. HUDDLESTON, assistant superintendent of the Northern California & Nevada District, Assemblies of God

Manny Mill is truly a diamond in God's jewelry box. The world rarely sees what God can do with a life that is totally surrendered. In Manny Mill, we are blessed to see this transformation that we read about in God's Word so beautifully displayed.

—ROBERT TONEY, chaplain supervisor, Louisiana State Penitentiary, Angola, LA

I experience the radical redemption of my dear brother Manny Mill every time I come into contact with him, whether it be in personal fellowship, ministry business, or as we serve together in the prisons. Galatians 2:20 is truly a living reality in this man, as I see Jesus living in and through him. Manny Mill is "the real deal" and I count it a great honor and privilege to know him!

—BOB WOLFSON, Cook County Jail Ministry;
Koinonia House National Ministries Board
Member; Attorney at Law/CPA

For every inmate he ministers to, Manny Mill becomes a beacon to freedom through Christ. This book will make it possible for EVERY inmate to know his story, their story—the story of redemption and the love of God for every person behind bars.

—TOM AND WENDY HORTON, volunteer
chaplains for the Illinois Department of Corrections; Prison and Justice Leaders, Willow Creek
Community Church

Manny Mill's infectious enthusiasm and deep sense of the sovereign grace of God propelled him into ground-breaking prison outreach within the state of Illinois. With characteristic, God-given passion and joy he visits his brothers in prison and inspires others to join him in this ministry. His visits to Angola Prison in Louisiana inspired him to encourage Christian men to found a theological seminary within an Illinois Correctional Center. The result is that men who Manny mentored founded Divine Hope Reformed Bible Seminary, a four-year theological seminary within the Danville Correctional Center. Manny continues his trailblazing work by hosting intensive three-day evangelistic and teaching retreats throughout correctional centers in Illinois.

—NATHAN BRUMMEL, professor of theology,
Divine Hope Reformed Bible Seminary

Manny has become a dear friend and partner to our ministry as we have adopted him as our evangelist. We work closely together as partners for the gospel of Christ. He is an amazing, GENUINE man of God who is sound in doctrine and committed to the TRUTH. Manny is the real deal.

—**CHUCK BABB**, pastor of CrossPointe Fellowship Church: Elizabethton, TN

Wow! That is the response that comes to mind when I think of Manny Mill. *Radical Redemption* is not just the title of a book, but it accurately characterizes the life of Manny Mill. Manny is a preacher, teacher, scholar, author, brother, friend, and mentor. Manny's life is a tangible demonstration of the grace of Jesus Christ. Manny's energy and passion to demonstrate and deliver the gospel to those who are often forgotten is untiring, unrelenting, and always challenging. My father and I have had the privilege to serve alongside Manny throughout the country. The love and humility that he demonstrates to everyone he meets is unforgettable and inspiring.

—**JEFF AND HEITH REYNOLDS**, father and son ministry team, pastors, Lost Creek Ministries, Wise, VA

Manny Mill's story is a powerful testimony of God's goodness and grace. If you have not yet had the experience of hearing Manny preach the gospel in person, this book will be a great first introduction. Manny's passion for Christ reflects the passion Christ had for Manny when he rescued him from a life headed 100 miles an hour in the wrong direction.

—**JOHN BYRNE**, regional executive director, Prison Fellowship MN, SD, ND

I am blessed to call Manny and Barbara Mill my friends and co-laborers behind prison walls for Christ. The message and messenger have brought hope and restoration to many broken lives. Our offender population has a term of endearment that they have given to Manny and the Koinonia House Ministry team; they are known as "the real deal." It is with great anticipation and a sense of deep urgency that we await the much-needed release of *Radical Redemption* in Spanish and the prison version to our population.

—STEPHEN C. KEIM, chief chaplain,
Illinois Department of Corrections

I first met Manny Mill at the Institute of Holy Land Studies on Mt. Zion in Jerusalem in 1989. He is a man who has been transformed by the grace and power of Christ. In the fall of 2012 he came to my hurting home-town and delivered a series of messages that bridged both ethnic and denominational divides. With genuine enthusiasm, Manny pointed the hearts of lost and lonely people to Jesus Christ.

—REV. PERRY E. MESSICK, First Baptist Church,
Collingdale, PA; chaplain—Law Enforcement
Chaplains of Delaware County (LECDC)

Manny Mill is the real deal. Manny is one of the most dynamic and entertaining speakers I know—a Bible-based Christian who hit bottom in prison and with grace vows to never return. Hear one of the world's best storytellers explain what the Lord has planned for you.

—MARK C. CURRAN JR., sheriff, Lake County, IL

To meet Manny Mill is to experience *Radical Redemption.* As a man he reflects holiness. As a husband and a dad he reveals self-sacrifice. In the prisons, he oozes with hope and restoration through Jesus as he teaches and spends time with those who are where he once was. As an ex-felon he is radically redeemed. In this book, he chronicles a journey from selfishness and crime to servanthood and holiness. Manny tells his story and it is a story we all need to hear.

—JIM LISKE, CEO, Prison Fellowship Ministries

Manny's story is a powerful testament to how a life can be thoroughly and dramatically transformed through the power of the Holy Spirit. He is a trophy in the Lord's conversion cabinet. Accompanying him on his first return to his homeland of Cuba in more than forty years, and watching him preach there, was life-changing for me.

—GEORGE L. ACOSTA, A/S Acosta & Skawski, PC

FOREWORD BY CHARLES COLSON

RADICAL
REDEMPTION

THE REAL STORY OF MANNY MILL

MANNY MILL

with Jude Skallerup

MOODY PUBLISHERS
CHICAGO

All Scripture quotations are taken from the *Holy Bible, New International Version*®. NIV®. Copyright © 1973, 1978, 1984 by International Bible Society. Used by permission of Zondervan Publishing House. All rights reserved.

Koinonia House® is a registered trademark of Charles Missler of Koinonia House®, Coeur d'Alene, Idaho. All rights reserved.

Portions of the dialogue in Chapter 5, *Radical Redemption*, were taken from the original script of *Unshackled!* program number 2468—Manny Mill, written by Kennetha Gaebler. *Unshackled!* is the radio drama from Pacific Garden Mission in Chicago. Used by permission.

Edited by Cheryl Dunlop
Cover Design: Kathryn Joachim   Interior Design: Ragont Design
Cover Image: iStock 2007 / Andrejs Zemdega
Author Photo: Jim Whitmer Photography

Library of Congress Cataloging-in-Publication Data

Mill, Manny.
    Radical redemption : the real story of Manny Mill /
Manny Mill with Jude Skallerup.
        p. cm.
    ISBN 0-8024-0883-9
    1. Mill, Manny. 2. Christian biography—United
States. I. Skallerup, Jude. II. Title.
BR1725.M444A3 2003
277.3'0825'092--dc21

                                                        2003009485

We hope you enjoy this book from Moody Publishers. Our goal is to provide high-quality, thought-provoking books and products that connect truth to your real needs and challenges. For more information on other books and products written and produced from a biblical perspective, go to www.moodypublishers.com or write to:

Moody Publishers
820 N. LaSalle Boulevard
Chicago, IL 60610

5 7 9 10 8 6 4

Printed in the United States of America

To the living memory of
the late Dr. Kenneth T. Wessner,
my friend, mentor, and spiritual daddy,
whose righteous legacy laid the foundation
for the writing of this story

Contents

Foreword

Manny Mill is one of the most exuberant and energetic human beings I have ever known. When I hear his name I think about God's great grace in lifting someone out of prison and then setting him forth on a magnificent mission. I think about energy, drive, commitment, and vision. Manny is nothing less than relentless; when he gets an idea it becomes a holy obsession. I just thank God that Christ has come to guide him and direct him and use him so powerfully.

I first met Manny when he was a prisoner and came to Washington as part of our In-prison Discipleship Program. We used to bring groups of inmates out for two weeks, train them, help them experience real Christian fellowship,

✦ ✦

teach them how to relate to other inmates, and then put them back in their prisons. It was a wonderful ministry but high cost, and so we have since discontinued it. We had hundreds of inmates come out during the ten or twelve years that we did this. And a few of them went on to become real leaders. None has distinguished himself more than Manny.

I remember him as an excited, enthusiastic young man, whom we immediately picked as one who had a bright future, who would become a leader. Little did we expect him to do the great things he has done with a ministry to ex-prisoners. Koinonia House is a family-home-based ministry of biblical discipleship for Christians coming out of prison, and it began only two years after Manny's release from prison.

Manny always makes an impression. I can remember sitting on the platform with ten thousand people in attendance in Amsterdam for Amsterdam 2000, Billy Graham's outreach to third-world evangelists. I was getting ready to speak, and just before I was introduced I felt someone grab me from behind and give me a kiss. It was Manny, who was praying for me throughout the speech and cheering me on with encouraging expressions.

So many places that I have visited and traveled to, Manny has been there. This man really has boundless energy. When he sets his mind to something, he does not look back, he moves out. He would have been a great Marine officer.

The great satisfaction I have is pouring my life into other people and seeing them pick up the cause and carry on God's work in the neediest places. Manny is indeed a wonderful living monument of God's grace in my life. If I could, I'd reproduce him. If I had a hundred Manny Mills going out across the country, there's no telling what would happen for the Kingdom.

Manny (and Barbara as well) has a tremendous heart. There's no way a person could do what he does, caring for those coming out of prison, if he wasn't overflowing with love. Along with this remarkable drive and enthusiasm, he is a guy who has a passionate love affair with Christ and a passionate love affair with people in trouble. He really cares about others.

Anyone who reads Manny's story is going to be blessed, because this is a terrific testimony of God's grace. You are going to see a story of a man who has overcome handicaps, disabilities, and a troubled past to become a great witness for Christ and a great servant. You are going to be moved by the example of his accomplishments and by his indomitable spirit. This is a story that will appeal to people in every walk of life, and of course it will have a special appeal to inmates and give them hope that if Manny could make it they can make it as well.

God found an ordinary Cuban man, Manny Mill, and Jesus made Manny extraordinary. By reading this story, you will get to know Manny and some of the characters who shaped his life, especially his wife, Barbara. As you experience his laughter, his joy, his passion, and at times his tears, my prayer is that you will also experience a deeper love for the Lord Jesus Christ who radically changes lives.

CHARLES W. COLSON
Founder, Prison Fellowship Ministries

Meeting
MANNY MILL

M ANNY LIKES TO EAT bananas with pizza. I just found that out recently. In all the times we've eaten pizza together (thank you, Domino's Pizza, for your generous discounts), I never noticed him doing that. It doesn't surprise me, though. Cubans love plantains, a particular type of banana plant. They cook it several ways and eat it as a side dish with just about any entrée. My own personal favorite is the fried sweet plantain called *maduros,* and my son, James, loves the crispy, salty banana chips called *mariquitas.* Even black beans and rice have a whole new meaning, now that I've eaten them with Manny.

There's something special about eating with Manny. It doesn't really matter what's on the menu. Manny and I have been on the receiving end of some fabulous feasts, and we've shared leftover leftovers while working through lunch in his office. We laugh a lot, for sure, but I can't imagine having a superficial meal with him. Some kind of meaningful exchange is habitually a part of the meal. He has a way of connecting with people that is as natural as eating itself— but he wasn't always like that.

The real story of Manny Mill includes more danger and adventure than most of us watch in a lifetime of movies. Much of it happened to Manny before he became a Christian, but nothing in his prior life was as challenging as the circumstances he faced as a student at Wheaton College. I worked at the college then, and I remember being concerned for him. He was older than most of his fellow students but young in years as a Christian. He had only lived as a Christian behind bars, not in the world. He was so Cuban and so clueless about how to function in that new environment.

After graduate school, Manny and Barbara, his wife, began a ministry for ex-prisoners. The two things about Manny that compelled me to join their ministry team were his passionate love for Jesus and his intentional effort to draw people of color into the work of the ministry. My Jewish identity seemed to delight Manny more than it delighted me. I was genuinely comfortable with his Cuban mannerisms, particularly

his speaking volume. In my family, loudness often represented conflict, but with Manny, the
volume usually characterized joy. I had no problem adjusting to that, and God gave me a super-
natural gift of interpretation when it came to his
Spanglish way of expressing himself.

That's how I came to be the one to "translate"
Manny's story for you. I must confess, the hardest
part was trying to capture on paper the man I
never knew, the old Manny Mill. Consequently, I
began the story with getting to know Manny's
Cuban family, catching the flavor of his life in
Cuba and his family's struggle for freedom.

So grab a *sombrero*, because it's sunny and
hot where we are going. Bring your tour guide,
too, as we start this story in a land that's close to
North America in miles but very far away from
the experience of most of us. It makes the rest
of the story much more meaningful.

The transforming power of a radical redemption is clearly evident in the contrast of
who Manny was and who he is today.

I hope you enjoy the journey at least as
much as I enjoyed its writing.

JUDE SKALLERUP

•

Introduction

JOYFUL DEBTOR. Creative *koinonia*. These
two phrases characterize the ten years of my
life since the first edition of *Radical Redemption*
was released.

Koinonia is a Greek word most often trans-
lated in English as "fellowship." But the meaning
goes much deeper than just socializing with others. True *koinonia* involves a partnership, a working toward a common goal. And in the Christian
community it involves mutually encouraging one
another in our faith in Jesus Christ.

By the grace of God, the Koinonia House®
National Ministries team and I have been involved in unique and creative collaborations,
true *koinonia* resulting in greater awareness of
the complexities and blessings of both in-prison

and postprison ministry and in lives transformed for the glory of God.

In the fall of 2003, through truly providential circumstances, I invited the leaders of Awana®, an international children's ministry, to accompany me on a visit to the Louisiana State Penitentiary at Angola. Why invite a children's ministry to an adult male prison? Knowing that children of inmates are seven times more likely than other children to become inmates themselves, I believed that if these leaders could spend just a little time with those inmates who were Christians and hear the cry of their hearts concerning their children, something good would come of it. And something did.

Awana's Lifeline™ ministry, sprouting from a special one-day event for inmates and their children in this one prison, spread to many more prisons. Lifeline™ eventually expanded to local churches and community-based groups, seeking to equip fathers, incarcerated or free, to build a legacy of faith in Christ Jesus.

Whenever a fifth Sunday occurs in a month, you will find volunteers associated with Koinonia House National Ministries worshiping with the men at Danville Correctional Center, a medium-security facility in Illinois. Because the prison is located about 160 miles from our ministry's headquarters in Wheaton, the ministry team needs to assemble in the driveway at 3:30 a.m.

to begin our drive to the prison.

A neighbor noticed the group one Sunday and approached me the next day asking if I had taken a group fishing. Of course, in the neighbor's mind, why else would men be gathering *that* early on a *Sunday* morning? "Yes," I replied, "just as Jesus said, we are fishers of men!" The man was surprised to learn that people would voluntarily get up so early to drive to a prison "just to have church." As a result of this conversation, this faithful group was nicknamed "The Fifth Sunday Fishermen." Sadly, the neighbor didn't have eyes of faith; he couldn't see what I saw.

I saw, I knew that more than "just church" was taking place. Biblical truths were being proclaimed. Lives were being transformed. Christian inmates were being discipled. Ministry relationships were being built. Volunteers' views of inmates were being challenged. And the seeds for two other ministries were being planted.

Derek, a devoted follower of Jesus Christ and a leader in the prison church, had already been incarcerated for four years when I first met him in Danville in 1993. Over the next eleven years, the Fifth Sunday Fishermen developed a relationship with Derek through worship services, weekend seminars, and correspondence. In 2004, he sought my help as he prepared for his release and return to society. Although Derek

was an excellent candidate for the Koinonia
House of Wheaton, his offense made him in-
eligible to reside there. My response to this
dilemma was, "Let's get creative!"

Bill, recently released from prison himself
and newly involved with Koinonia House National Ministries, invited Derek to share his two-
bedroom apartment. First Presbyterian Church
of Glen Ellyn, Illinois, arranged for mentors to
meet weekly with Derek and provided families
to host him on Sundays after church. Daily discipleship classes were taught by the Discipleship and Resident Directors at the Koinonia
House® of Wheaton. Employment was secured
through the network of relationships within the
ministry.

Today, Derek and his wife are very active in
their local church, and Derek is an official volunteer chaplain for the Illinois Department of Corrections (IDOC)—even returning to Danville to
proclaim the good news of Jesus Christ as a
"Fifth Sunday Fisherman." Through creative
koinonia, Christians working together in mutual
partnership, Derek made a successful transition
back to society.

This creative solution grew into the Meet
Me at the Gate® initiative. Through formal
Meet Me at the Gate training workshops or in-
formal networking in response to an individual
plea for help, we equip local churches to come

alongside those Christians being released from prison who do not have access to a postprison residential program. In the last ten years, Meet Me at the Gate training and networking has taken place throughout Illinois and in several other states.

The second seed of ministry took longer to germinate. Initially, most of the Fifth Sunday Fishermen came from the Wheaton, Illinois, area. But over the last decade, the majority of volunteers have been members of United Reformed churches in northwest Indiana. I was greatly impressed by this group's consistency in serving at the prison and challenged them to take the next step and meet a Christian brother at the Danville Correctional Center gate.

While the volunteers excitedly took up my challenge, they soon faced another. The prison was located in Illinois; their churches were located just across the border in Indiana. The men could not be paroled across state lines. Wanting to help the prison church with whom they had labored over ten years, but unable to do so through the Meet Me at the Gate initiative, it was time for another creative solution to the need for biblical discipleship. The seeds of theological education behind bars began to take root.

Once again, I used a trip to the Louisiana State Penitentiary at Angola as a nursery for this new ministry seedling. Warden Burl Cain graciously arranged for the men from northwest Indiana and IDOC officials to tour the Angola satellite campus of the New Orleans Baptist Seminary. There they learned firsthand of the positive impact the educational program has had not only in the lives of the individual students but on the prison as a whole.

Returning to Indiana, the group dug in and went to work. In the spring of 2012, the Divine Hope Reformed Bible Seminary was inaugurated at the Danville Correctional Center with close to thirty students beginning a study of the doctrine of God. Once again, creative koinonia resulted in lives transformed by the power of Jesus Christ.

And lives transformed by the power of Jesus Christ are what I'm all about. Like the Apostle Paul (an accomplice to murder in at least one person's death [see Acts 7:54–8:1]), I boldly proclaim that I am "not ashamed of the gospel, because it is the power of God for the salvation of everyone who believes: first for the Jew, then for the Gentile. For in the gospel a righteousness from God is revealed, a righteousness that is by faith from first to last . . ." (Romans 1:16–17 NIV).

This glorious gospel causes me to be a joyful debtor. I am not a debtor to the grace of God, for God does not require repayment. Besides being impossible to repay, any effort would be a work on our part, and grace is all of God. Rather, I see myself, again like the Apostle Paul, as a joyful debtor "both to Greeks and to barbarians, both to the wise and to the foolish" (Romans 1:14 NASB). Barbarian and foolish may well be how many people today think of those incarcerated behind prison walls. Greek (or well-educated) and wise may describe others who are not incarcerated in physical prisons yet are enslaved by sin. I consider myself a joyful debtor to both, eager to share the gospel with all.

Manny Mill

God blessed my eagerness to share the gospel, and in these last ten years opened doors for ministry that I could never have imagined. I have preached in churches and prisons across the United States. I have been interviewed for numerous print publications and radio and television programs. Internationally, I have ministered in Canada, Costa Rica, Mexico, Brazil, and Uganda. In 2010, God even opened the doors for me to return to Cuba, where I had the extraordinary privilege of preaching at a church in my childhood *barrio*.

In addition to being indebted to those who have not heard the gospel, I consider myself indebted to all those whom God has brought into my life to encourage me in my faith. You will meet many of them in the following pages. One special brother in Christ was Chuck Colson, founder of Prison Fellowship. I was in Kampala, Uganda, preparing to speak at the Luzira National Prison, when I learned that Chuck had died. In the following days, as numerous memories of interactions with Chuck flooded my mind, so did the text of Hebrews 13:7, "Remember those who led you, who spoke the word of God to you; and considering the result of their conduct, imitate their faith" (NASB).

The command of Hebrews 13:7 is to imitate the faith of others, not their achievements or activities but their faith. The following story of radical redemption tells how I came to faith in Christ Jesus through the grace of God alone, how I became a joyful debtor and began a life of creative koinonia for the joy and benefit of many —and all for the glory of God.

1

•

Life in
CUBA

WHAT DO YOU THINK of when you hear the word "Cuba"? Do you think of Fidel Castro? Or, if you are old enough, the Bay of Pigs or the Cuban Missile Crisis? My children might remember the little boy, Elián González, who lost his mother while fleeing Cuba and became a national icon as government leaders debated where he should live. I can relate to that little boy. I love my Cuban family and my homeland, but I cannot forget the suffering that still exists there today.

In 1956, the year I was born, Cuba was a popular place for a weekend getaway. From Key West, Florida, to Havana was a ninety-mile trip across the Straits of Florida. Wealthy people put their cars on a ferry, rode over for a weekend of drinking, gambling, and carousing, and then rode back. Most tourists were not interested in the Cubans east of Havana, living in straw huts with no running water or electricity. Illiteracy was high, and about 25 percent of the country's adult males were unemployed. Fulgencio Batista was the dictator then, and he was involved in a lot of corruption. A familiar story, yes? The need for change was obvious, so many people were glad when Fidel Castro came down from his rebel headquarters in the mountains on January 1, 1959. At age thirty-three, he had defeated Batista. A white dove on his shoulder, a Cuban cigar in his mouth, a long beard on his face, and the strength of his resolve gave the impression that he was a type of savior for the Cuban people. I was three years old.

My Family

My grandparents, Manolo Mill Hernandez and Rafaela Hernandez Hernandez de Mill, moved from a little town called Sagua La Grande, in the Cuban province of Las Villas, in 1927, when my father was about two. They settled in a suburb of Havana called Santos Suárez, which was also where I was born, and they owned a little cigar factory in the back of their house. Cuban children are given two last names, their father's and their mother's, and it is always the paternal name from each parent. Manolo and Rafaela had three children, Rafael Mill Hernandez, Nora Mill Hernandez, and my father, Manolo Mill Hernandez.

My dad, *mi viejo* as I called him, worked extraordinarily hard. He looked just like me. I guess I should say that I look like him. He was a very active man, driven to provide for his family. Even as a young boy, he helped my grandfather with the cigar business by making most of the deliveries. Cigars in hand, walking wherever they had to be delivered, there went little seven-year-old Manolo Mill. After about the sixth grade, he quit school, and he worked from that time on. The desire to work was instilled in him, and he transferred it to me. Later, perhaps by age eighteen or twenty, Manolo followed in his brother Rafael's footsteps and became a butcher.

I affectionately address Uncle Rafael as *Tío Tato*. The Spanish word for uncle is *tío,* and the word *tato* is a word of endearment that I only use for him, like Dearest Uncle. Tío Tato lived in Cuba and worked as a butcher in his hometown, Lawton. He is retired now because of blindness and still lives in Lawton.

His sister, my aunt Nora, Tía Nora, is a medical doctor, a gynecologist. She was married to another doctor, Dr. José Fernandez Echazabal, who was my Tío Pepé. Pepé is the nickname for José. In Cuba, when a woman marries, she does not take the name of her husband. Instead, she adds it onto the end, like she "belongs to" her husband, so Tía Nora's full name was Nora Mill Hernandez de Echazabal. Tía Nora and Tío Pepé had two daughters, Silvita, who became a dentist, and Norita, who became a psychologist.

Tío Pepé was the head of Hospital Aballí, a hospital for children in Havana. He was a well-known pediatrician and allergist in Cuba, a brilliant man who had been schooled in New York. He was a very important person in my life, like a daddy to me. We spent a lot of time together fishing or at beach clubs. I never sat above water and fished with a fishing pole. We fished by snorkeling or scuba diving and using harpoons and knives. My parents included me in their leisure activities, but Tío Pepé was the one who took me all kinds of places. Because he had a lot of clout, we were able to go to spots that were normally just for foreigners, like Club Americano, where we played racquetball together. We swam in luxurious pools and ate in the best restaurants all over the island, even under Communist rule. He had a 1960 Chevy Impala in mint condition. We spent great times together in that car.

Tía Nora eventually divorced him, because he was a womanizer, and his example strongly influenced my own behavior when I grew up. One day a bus struck Tío Pepé and badly injured his legs, requiring emergency surgery. In spite of his renowned reputation, no penicillin was available for him. All the money in the world couldn't buy what they didn't have, and Tío Pepé died of infection.

Because professional people were not allowed to leave Cuba, after her divorce Tía Nora arranged a marriage with a Cuban political prisoner who spent more than twenty years in prison. He was released as part of a deal the U.S. made with Cuba in the 1980s. Since he was allowed to leave and she was married to him, she and my two cousins got out of Cuba and went to Miami. I don't know how much Tía Nora loved him then, but they remained married.

MY PARENTS

As a butcher in Cuba, my dad sold mostly beef. He did not slaughter animals himself. He received them whole, and then he had to cut the pieces. La Carniceria, the meat store, was about twenty minutes from our house, in another suburb called La Víbora. The store was in a busy location, right next to a bus terminal, Paradero de la Víbora, in Havana, and not too far from the Clinica Lourdes where I was born. There was also a university right behind the *clinica,* so this tiny little store saw a lot of action selling just meat.

My mother, Norma Martinez Ochoa, first met my father at a party given to celebrate the end of a school year. They were at El Centro Dependiente, kind of like a banquet hall. My mom, *mi vieja*, was fifteen or sixteen years old at that time. They hit it off really well. Dad said he wanted to continue seeing her, but Mom was shy about it. This would be her first relationship with a young man, and she thought that giving him her address was inappropriate. In those days, women were very discreet in the way they approached relationships. Mom lived with her aunt, so while she and her aunt were walking home, Dad followed them in order to find out where she lived.

A trolley line passed right by Mom's house, and Dad told her that he was going to ride by. So she sat on the balcony and watched as he passed by on the trolley, waving to her. She knew that he liked her, and when he asked for her phone number, she allowed him to call. Then he asked if he could visit her. A month after he started visiting her, Dad made up his mind to ask for her hand in marriage. Altogether, it was three years from the time they met until they married on June 19, 1949. He was her only boyfriend, the only man in her life, and they celebrated fifty years together before Dad died and went to be with Jesus.

While they courted, Mom worked as a secretary for General Motors, but after they married, Dad didn't want her to work any longer. Because Mom liked to work, she thought of a way to do it at home in her living room. She started doing manicures and washing hair, just small stuff until her business grew. Then Dad built her a big beauty salon in front of their home on La Calle Rabí. In those days, men allowing their women to work outside the home was not common, but Dad recognized Mom's uncommon talent. She also worked for Channel Four Television, styling hair for Cuban entertainers and movie stars from the U.S.

A CUBAN CHILDHOOD

My parents were great financial providers. Since both were consumed by their work, I was raised by a *tata,* a nanny, who took good care of me. I remember going to the park, Parque Santo Súarez, named after the suburb of Havana where we lived. It was just a few blocks from my house, so my *tata* and I went every day and played.

All available relatives and other kids from the neighborhood enjoyed my traditional Cuban birthday parties, especially *la piñata.* Outings with my parents were most often to the shore, the beaches of Havana. My parents were members of a bank club called Santa María del Mar—St. Mary of the Sea—which had a very beautiful and exclusive beach. Extended family got together there on weekends, and sometimes my parents rented a house and stayed there for their vacation. Mom's first cousin, Rolando Ochoa Garcia, owned a beautiful home on another exclusive beach called Boca Ciega. The family got together there sometimes. Cousin Rolando was a comedian and an entertainer, like the Bob Hope of Cuba. He hosted a popular prime-time show on national TV, *El Cabaré de Regalía*. He left Cuba in 1960, shortly after Castro came to power.

My great-grandfather, my mom's grandfather, was a devout Roman Catholic and the only doctor in Regla/Casablanca, two cities in the province of Havana surrounded by water. We had to take a boat, *La Lanchita de Regla*, to visit his home. He was generous to the people he served. If they had no money to pay, he helped them at no charge. When he came from Spain, he brought a big statue of *La Virgen de Regla*, the Queen of the Sea. She had a 22-karat-gold-plated robe, and I remember her mostly because she was the saint of September 7, my birthday. My mom superstitiously taught me to stand at the edge of the shore with seven *centavos*, pennies, in my little hand and throw them into the sea, asking the queen for permission to go swimming and protection from drowning. She was the one to please, because I was born on her day.

When I was four years old, my sister, Normita Mill Martinez, was born. Besides the four of us, my mom's brother, René Martinez Ochoa, was the other close member of our family. My parents cared for Tío René all of his life.

My mom told me that I was a very orderly little boy. My toys were always all lined up and my room was very clean. She said I was so careful that when I finished playing, I put my toys back in their boxes just how they came. She said I was polite, never sassy to her, and never a loudmouth. I guess "loud" is a matter of perception!

My dad was a good man and I know he loved me. He was not a Christian believer yet, so of course, when I say he was good, I mean relatively moral, because he was a sinner. He was a law-abiding, decent man, providing for his family, but a sinner just the same. He had a genuine desire to provide for us the best he could, but he could not impart anything of eternal value, since he did not know Jesus during the years I lived with him. He did not even believe in God.

I don't really remember having a one-on-one talk with my dad about anything. He just basically allowed me to see the way he lived and I caught what I could from that. Without the fear of God, I was not able to get a strong sense of right and wrong.

RELIGIOUS TRAINING IN CUBA

I attended a Roman Catholic school, La Escuela de Las Pias, until Castro took over everything, and then I attended "Castro school" where they indoctrinated us in the Communist system. Although God was not a part of that system, *santería* (witchcraft) was. Castro himself was very involved in witchcraft, as were many Cubans, including my own mom, who practiced *espiritismo,* spiritism, and became a medium.

Most Cubans prayed to statues of the Roman Catholic saints as a part of witchcraft practices, offering apples, coconuts, and even cigars to gain their favor. The requests were usually self-serving, either for personal gain or harm to an enemy. The Roman Catholic Church leaders misled the Cuban people because they condoned these practices and did not speak out against them as they should have. Church leaders emphasized attendance on Easter and Christmas, but the rest of the year it seemed OK to do whatever one wanted. Cubans had difficulty understanding the need to come to Christ, because they thought they already knew God. Their ungodly religious practices clouded the truth of the gospel.

La Escuela de Las Pias had kindergarten through eighth grade, and it was run by nuns. Their clothing fascinated me. Yards of fabric flowed all the way down to their feet. I was so intrigued with what was under there that my curiosity drove me to do a terrible thing. From behind one nun, I went under her dress, touching her legs to see some skin. I wanted to see her thighs. I guess that was the start of my womanizing lifestyle to come. My first attraction to a female and she was a nun! She took me to the principal's office and had my mom come to school and rescue me. I think my inner sense of morality went downhill from that day on.

Generally speaking, teachers told my mom that I was a good student and everything was fine. I was very organized like my dad. He was rigorous about order and doing all things well. He was also very concerned about my manhood, so he emphasized my participation in sports. Dad used to get upset when I played with my sister and her "girly" toys. My parents hoped to have children right away, but God didn't send me until eight years after they were married. Having waited so long for a son only put more emphasis on my need to be a man!

At age ten or eleven, Cuban students had to do "volunteer" work. So the government sent my whole class to the fields, supervised by schoolteachers. We went for two months away from home, to do anything that we could—pick tomatoes, pick bananas, help in the field, whatever. We had to give that time to Castro's government system of Communism. We slept on bunks without a mattress or a pillow, in burlap sackcloth. The food was terrible, the conditions were terrible, and the work was hard. Some people think that with Communism everything was free. That was not true, because we worked for it. The military was involved as well, combined with the school personnel, and they let us know who was in charge. It was a dictatorship; we knew we had better do what they said.

Once a male child reached age fifteen, he was obligated to register for El Servicio Militar Obligatorio, military service, and at age sixteen he enlisted. The government did not allow registered persons to leave Cuba, so as I grew up the window of opportunity was closing on getting out of Cuba. My mom continued to press my dad about leaving, because by the time a young man turned fourteen, if he hadn't already gotten out, he probably would not make it.

SPORTS AND MY WHOLE HEART

Just before we left as refugees when I was fourteen, I was awarded a black belt in judo. I had a great judo professor, El Loco Valdés, and he was crazy like his name. Once he fought a gorilla, just to be able to tell people how good he was. So he was crazy, I mean a gutsy, daring kind of crazy guy. He was the only Cuban black belt in judo and either fourth or fifth dan (degree). That meant he was really up there, a top guy in his weight. He was in a league all by himself, and he was my judo professor for about eight years.

He was tough with us, but very practical. He would tell us, "If you are going to fight in the street, you won't have a mattress." Many days at judo practice he made us break our fall on the concrete floor, just to get used to it. Of course, at first we were aching in pain. It was not the same as breaking our fall on a mat, which was pretty comfortable. Nevertheless, we did get used to it. Some nights we had no mat and no light, because of *el pico eléctrico,* certain times when the government cut the electricity to save energy. El Loco Valdés had us practice with a flashlight. And when we didn't have a flashlight, we practiced with a match. Can you imagine that? With a match. He was a tough guy, but he really taught us a lot of good stuff about discipline, keeping our word, and being on time. He was no-nonsense about the time. We had to be on time, all the time.

When I was a yellow belt, not too many years into judo, I was at a competition and got thrown. I landed very wrong, on my stomach, and it knocked the wind out of me. I couldn't breathe at all, and there was El Loco Valdés by the sideline telling me, "Get up! Get up! Go back to the mat." He had no mercy. Talk about pushing somebody past his limit. He basically turned me into a man, because he had no mercy whatsoever.

I was about six or seven when I started judo. I was small, and I stuttered profusely. A lot of people made fun of me, but after a while, they couldn't make fun of me anymore, at least not without a fight. I was very well-behaved in school, but I would point to a fellow student and say, "I'll see *you* after school!" Then in the street, I would pound on the kid. I got some beatings, too, but I was always fighting.

In the States, I became known as a baseball player, but that was my least favorite sport in Cuba. I learned ping-pong from the Chinese, holding the racket their way, allowing more flexibility and quicker moves. I liked volleyball almost as much as ping-pong, and strove to be good at both. I was not tall, so I wasn't a volleyball spiker, but I was a good set-up man. I was very smooth. I had a good serve from on top or from the bottom and was good with my fingertips. I had the touch.

Sports became a big deal under Castro's rule, and every kid wanted to be in sports. There was great incentive to make the national sports teams, because they traveled outside Cuba. Team members were allowed to buy things in foreign countries that they could never get at home. It was a coveted privilege to bring things back for themselves and their families.

All the schools competed against the one elite school called ESPAD where the best of the best of the kids in any sport attended. Whether it was ping-pong, volleyball, baseball, basketball, or fencing, kids in all the schools competed and hoped to beat the kids from ESPAD. Winning meant an automatic scholarship to go into ES-PAD, and I used to beat those kids in ping-pong. But I was a marked man, a *gusano*. A person who wanted to leave Cuba was called a *gusano*, like a worm. Being a worm was something like being considered a traitor. Because of that, I was excluded from getting a scholarship.

Sports taught me a lot about discipline, and the demand to compete in Cuba taught me how to approach competition. No halfheartedness was in me at all. This drive that swelled inside me as a young teenager would serve me well in the challenging days ahead.

Living in Cuba was difficult after Castro came into power. My family had been accustomed to a very comfortable lifestyle, and then everything changed. Things had to be done in secret. No one, including my dad, could be open anymore about anything. Castro and his government commandeered everything without any compensation in return, including my dad's meat store and my mom's beauty salon. That's when my dad could no longer ignore the pleas of my mom to leave Cuba.

2

◆

Narrow
ESCAPES

WHEN MAO TSE-TUNG took over China in 1949, many Chinese had already fled from Communism there and come to Cuba, so many kids my age were second- or third-generation Chinese-Cuban. One of my parents' Chinese friends commented, "I escaped China, running from Mao Tse-tung, and look what happened. Here I am with Castro. Now I'm going to the U.S.A., and if Communism comes there, I guess I will just go down," meaning he would give up and die, having nowhere else to go.

Naturally, I was introduced to Chinese food at an early age. My dad loved to eat lunch at *la fonda China,* a tiny, family-owned Chinese restaurant right in the neighborhood. In Spanish, *fonda* means fly on the wall. It was a corner store, a hole-in-the-wall kind of place where the food was great. The menu was a combination of Chinese and Cuban food, demonstrating the owners' acculturation into Cuban life. These were hard-working people, like my dad, working from early morning until late in the evening.

Many of the Chinese-Cubans who fled to the United States settled in the Cuban neighborhoods of Miami, Florida, or Union City, New Jersey, even though there were many Chinese-American neighborhoods they could have chosen. Many Russians were also in Cuba, either going to school or teaching the Cubans technical skills. The Cuban economy received substantial financial support from the Soviet Union, until the union fell. Africans were already in Cuba, a result of the Spanish slave trading, so there was a great mix of cultures, and interracial marriages were common. All Cubans shared equally in the oppressive conditions.

EYES OF THE GOVERNMENT

On every block there was a family chosen by Castro's government who served on the Comité de Defensa de la Revolución (CDR). They acted as the eyes of the government, but they were more like snitches. We referred to them rather coldly as "the CDR," and it was no secret who they were. They were required to have a big sign in the front window of their home. In the beautiful building on the street where we lived, 52nd Calle Santa Irene, there were only three families. We had the first-floor apartment, with a beautiful corner balcony, and, in God's providence, right above us lived the CDR family for our block.

In order to gain points with the CDR, people became street spies and reported back to the CDR. Gaining points meant extra food and extra privileges. Those people were more secret and harder to detect.

Everyone had *la libreta,* the book. It was a rations booklet where we recorded the provisions we received. We were not permitted to go to the store and buy whatever we wanted to buy. Only so many pounds of rice a month, so many ounces of meat—ounces, not pounds. Ounces, per family. No milk like we have in the U.S.; ours was powdered milk, and only so much per month. So much cheese, so much this, so much that. It was really tough. Like many others, my dad dealt on the black market, and if he got caught, he would face prison time for sure. Having the CDR right upstairs meant we had to be very careful about how much we used the black market. We had to be careful even with what we talked about at home. We knew they could hear us. We didn't know how much, but they could hear. And we were *gusanos,* thought to be against the system, because we were planning to leave.

I was about eight years old when the Communists came into my dad's meat store one day and announced, "This is ours now. From today on, you work for us. You get ninety pesos a month." My dad was used to making one thousand pesos a month as the owner. He went from owner to government worker with no warning. Just like that. So, he began very carefully to steal meat from his meat store. It was tricky, because he had to account for all the sales. And he didn't want his CDR neighbors to notice how much meat his family ate.

Cuban citizens were "checked" or searched any time a government agent or CDR chose to do so. No search warrant was needed, no court orders, and searches were made for no apparent reason. Any package, any time. It was a very intrusive system. Talk about being on the edge. Every day that my dad carried meat home in a package, he wondered when he might get caught. There was no peace. No peace whatsoever.

Not long after we lost the meat store, the Communists took Mom's beauty salon. She was unwilling to work for the government, so she chose to quit. She went back to doing some work at home, on the side, but that had to be done carefully, because privatization was now against the law. Mom knew when to sneak people into the house and when to have them leave.

GETTING OUT OF CUBA

We all lived under these conditions for several years while my dad concentrated on preparations to leave Cuba. This sounds easier than it was. A string of impossible conditions had to be met in order to make it out. We had to declare that we were leaving in order to purchase airline tickets. We had to already have the funds in order to officially declare, and the funds had to be in U.S. dollars. However, possession of U.S. currency was illegal in Cuba, and exchanging Cuban pesos for U.S. dollars was called *tráfico de divisas,* trafficking U.S. money, punishable with imprisonment.

Again, my dad had to become creative in order to get around the domineering system. By the late 1960s, flights from Havana to Miami were closed. The only viable way out was through Madrid, Spain. KLM was the airline that provided flights from Havana. We had to buy round-trip tickets, nearly $500 each, and there were five of us, making the goal about $2,400.

So why buy round-trip tickets, since everyone knew we were leaving and not coming back? The full price had to be sent from the bank in Miami to Banco Nacional, the Cuban Bank owned by Castro. He paid KLM for one-way tickets and kept the rest. Only government officials used round-trip tickets. They had to come back. The government made sure, by keeping their families behind.

Mom's cousin Rolando Ochoa was hated by the Cuban government, especially by Castro, because he was one of the few people who saw Castro's real intentions early on. That is why he left Cuba with his family. His radio broadcasts from Miami bombarded Castro, but Castro couldn't do anything about it. Rolando was willing to serve as a bank for us in the U.S. He and Dad would make deals with families in Miami. If they gave a dollar for us to Rolando in the U.S., Dad gave seven Cuban pesos to a relative of that family still living in Cuba. These transactions were set up through the mail, using elaborate codes. Naturally, most mail was checked and read, especially if it came from a hated guy like Rolando Ochoa.

Dad was suspected of trafficking money and put in prison for a year. In Cuba, the accused are treated as guilty until the government decides otherwise. When my dad's letters to and from cousin Rolando were examined, there was no evidence of guilt. Even so, he was sent home on house arrest for another year, where he continued soliciting dollars until he had the funds to declare that we were leaving. Then Dad served two years in the Cuban fields working for Castro as a punishment for declaring.

I went to see my dad while he was in prison. He lost forty pounds in the first couple months. The only food he was given was the same stuff they gave cows. We were allowed to bring him whatever we could fit in one bag about once every six weeks.

FINALLY OUT

Even the smallest purchases were regulated, so airline tickets were highly supervised. Only *gusanos* were allowed to buy tickets, and even after all conditions were met, there was no guarantee that we would make it out. The government thought they held all the power, but the mercy of God was with us when we finally left Cuba.

KLM canceled its flight at the last minute. The five of us—Dad, Mom, Tío René, my sister Normita, and me—boarded a broken-down old plane owned by the Cubana de Aviación that was about to fall out of the sky. We spent eighteen hours traveling from Havana to Madrid, with an emergency landing on Azores Island, near Portugal, in the middle of the night when one of the engines failed. Even my big, strong father was sweating bullets over that one, but finally we landed in Spain, on November 14, 1970, refugees with nothing but the clothes on our backs.

We spent twenty-one months in Madrid. Dad worked all day long, but he made very little money. We ate at a refugee dining room, about an eight-block walk from the pension where we lived, and we still had to borrow money to afford these meager living conditions. Dad kept very meticulous records of how much each person sent, and when we got to the States he made sure that each one was paid back in full.

There were many Cuban families in Spain, all hoping to earn enough to pay for passage to the U.S. I was part of a group of young Cubans that hung out together. We had a lot of parties, because refugee kids were not allowed to attend school, and we had to do something together. One of our favorite groups was the Beatles, and my favorite song was *Please Mr. Postman*. And many of us worked. My first full-time job was at a shoe store as a salesman, and for one hour each day, I cleaned the store windows. I also helped my mom and dad, who were both employed in a beauty salon that sold wigs. Dad was bald, so he was the wig model, and Mom was the beautician. One of my jobs was to promote the salon, so I had a route I traveled every day for an hour or so, passing out flyers. My parents' earnings combined were five thousand *pecetas* a month. At seventy *pecetas* per dollar, that was about seventy-two dollars a month—not much money. I made twenty dollars a month at the shoe store.

None of us kids knew God. We thought we did, but our goal was to have a good time. Our group became really tight, hanging out together for nearly two years. I became very close with a young woman named Daisy. Her family also planned to come to the U.S., but when they could, no one knew. I did not like leaving her behind when we moved.

In the U.S.

Our destination was Atlanta, Georgia. My first job in the U.S. was as a busboy, and I worked hard at it. I was going to school full-time, working part-time, and helping my mom and dad financially. I still managed to save enough money in the first six months to go back to Spain and see Daisy. My dad thought I was crazy, but I got a visa, bought a ticket, and went back to Spain for two weeks. All my friends were still there, because we were one of the first families to leave. It was like a big reunion. And, of course, I spent time with Daisy. We were both sixteen and "in love."

Not long after I got back to the States, Daisy and her family moved to Queens, New York. We had been in Atlanta for about eleven months. I started talking about moving to Queens. My mom was not about to allow the family to split up, so I convinced my parents to move from

Atlanta to Queens, just because I wanted to be
with Daisy. We bought a beat-up old car, packed
our few little things, and drove to Queens. We
had never been on interstate highways before.
We bought a map and I acted as navigator,
which is a hilarious concept, since I don't know
north from south or east from west. By the grace
of God, I guided my parents, who did not speak
a word of English, and with my uncle and my
sister we made it to Queens. We moved into an
apartment right behind Macy's Department
Store, and we lived there three weeks. My dad
could not find any work.

One day, Dad took a drive through the Lincoln Tunnel from Manhattan into New Jersey,
which was just on the other side of the Hudson
River. He discovered a big Cuban community in
Union City, New Jersey. Man, was he excited! He
parked the car and went into a meat store, just
to check it out, since that had been his trade all
of his life. At one time, he was the president of
the Havana Butchers' Association. To my dad's
astonishment, the butcher inside recognized
him and enthusiastically blurted out, "Manolo,
what are you doin' here, Manolo?"

"Well, my son brought me to Queens. I am
looking for a job," my dad replied.

"You want to work?"

"Yeah!"

So the owner asked, "Manolo, how many

hours a day do you want to work?"

My dad's response was, "How many hours in a day? Twenty-four? I will work twenty-four."

"Manolo, how many days a week do you want to work?"

"How many days in a week? Seven? I will work seven."

My dad transferred to me that strong sense of responsibility to work. He continued to be driven to provide for his family, plus he had many debts to repay, so, of course, we moved again, to Union City. It was uncomfortable for my mom to have to move so much, but she willingly sacrificed for the benefit of the family.

3
◆

The American
DREAM

D AD TOOK THE JOB at the meat store in Union City, *Las Tres Hermanas,* The Three Sisters. He was a man of his word and worked seven days a week, seventeen hours a day, with one day off a year, Christmas. At the end of each day, he met a couple coworkers. They were dead tired, but to finish the day they shared a fifth of Jack Daniels and smoked Cuban cigars. I don't know how much he actually consumed, but I never saw him high or drunk or the least bit out of control. He came home, showered, ate, and went to sleep. Early the next morning, he would get up and do it all over again. He had a lot of energy, considering that he didn't sleep much.

He worked on his feet the whole day, even though he had a bad leg. Many years before, he had an accident. He was on a trolley in Havana and it was jam-packed, so he was hanging off the side in order to ride. When the electrical poles on the sidewalk became a threat, he had to choose between jumping off the car or smacking into a pole. He chose to jump and broke his left leg. He spent a long time in the hospital with nails and screws in his leg, and finally after a year it healed. He never complained about his leg— or anything else, for that matter.

BASEBALL DAYS

Not long after we moved, Daisy's family also moved to Union City. Then I dumped her and found somebody else. I had already enrolled in Union Hill High School as a junior. I made the baseball team, and, not long after, became team captain, all because of a customer from my dad's meat store named Pollo Rodríguez, one of Cuba's baseball legends. He was the best third baseman Cuba ever produced, and probably the best fake-bunt hitter that baseball ever produced.

Major League players in the U.S. do not know how to bunt the way Pollo did, and he taught me those skills. I was a hustler by nature, something the coach really liked, but I also had a skill that nobody else had. I held the bat with one hand on the handle and the other hand on the thick part, and made it look like a bunt. I stood with my feet spread apart, not one foot in front of the other. Then at the last second, I switched my hands. I had to see the pitch and make a decision if it was a good one. I had to be fast, bringing both hands together, pushing the ball right over third base. This caused confusion for the fielding team. The left fielder was back there, but the third baseman had moved forward. The short stop moved toward second base, the second baseman moved toward first base, and the first baseman moved forward, leaving a big hole just for my fake-bunt hit. And because I was fast and caught them off guard, I usually made it to second base.

I also faked when I was walked to first. As everybody talked out on the field, I trotted off casually to first base. Before they even noticed, I stole second base. That's what I meant when I said I was a hustler. Pollo taught me all that, the smart way to play baseball. I always talked out there while I played the field, trying to mess up the batters' concentration. Pollo called that *pimienta,* pepper, spicing up the game by moving around, talking to the pitcher, going to the mound to slap his behind, and all that. I yelled, "Swing!" to the batter, especially when our pitcher threw a bad one. It made the game unpredictable and more interesting, not really something that I found much here in the States, where baseball was more of a quiet game.

That was my ticket to college at Seton Hall

University in South Orange, New Jersey. Actually, I did not get a scholarship to Seton Hall, not right from high school. I was not that well-known in baseball. I had only played for two years at Union Hill, and usually the scouts wanted to watch a player all four years. I had to try out for the college team, and the competition was tough. Six or seven top players went after each position on Seton Hall's team. Once I made the team, then the financial aid and scholarship offices worked it out and gave me a full ride. I majored in women and minored in baseball.

DANCING NIGHTS

Anyone who was observing me would have decided my other minor was dancing. My real focus was self. Everything I did was always with me in mind, to better myself, to better my image, or to gain whatever I set my eyes on, which was usually a woman. Dancing was just the means to an end. I'm not even sure how I learned to dance. Just a natural gift, maybe. My sister was a great dancer, and my parents were too. I guess it ran in the family. I always enjoyed it, and I practiced a lot while I was living in Spain. When I grew older, I liked what dancing did for me.

In Union City, ballrooms and clubs were open every night with hot Cuban bands for dancing. If they happened to be closed, New York was only a short drive away. Every Wednesday night and every weekend, I went dancing. I was good and had fun doing it, so many women wanted to dance with me. I kept good rhythm and knew my steps, and I had hair back then! Cuban music is full of many different rhythms, different kinds of dances like the rumba, the cha-cha, the guaguanco, the mozambique, and the casino.

Rolandito Diaz came to Union City through Spain like I did, and his girlfriend, Teresita, was the daughter of my dad's partner at the meat store. Teresita and Rolandito were both fabulous dancers, so the three of us often went out together, recruiting other couples to dance rounds with us. Casino was a great synchronized dance, men tossing their partners around, using fancy steps. When we did rounds, we ruled the dance floor. Everybody stepped aside.

Basically I was the center of attention, which I thrived on, and I was in great shape. Dancing three or four times a week for hours at a time was serious exercise. I never stopped. When I went to dance, I was not interested in drugs or alcohol. My thing was women and dancing. I knew many people who did cocaine right there at the dance, and I saw it on the table. I never touched it, and I thank God that I didn't have to deal with drug addiction.

In most places, my cover charge was waived because I attracted so much business. The same

with the bar. Drinks for Manny Mill were free—
a no-risk proposition, since usually all I drank
was Coca Cola, and proprietors knew they
would profit plenty from everyone else I
brought. Once in a while I had a glass of wine
with dinner. I liked a particular German white
wine, but I never experienced intoxication until
I met the Holy Spirit many years later.

With that kind of social life, I began meeting lots of people in Union City. I was ambi-
tious, so I began promoting my own dances,
renting the hall, contracting the bands and
sometimes bartenders, the whole nine yards.
My first dance was in the gym at St. Joseph
High School in West New York, New Jersey. The
place was jam-packed. Some people could not
even get in. With the net profit from my first big
success, I paid cash for my first big car, a Lincoln Continental Mark IV.

Another Cuban guy named Manny, Manny
Diaz, also used to contract dances and shows.
When he noticed that this new kid on the block
could put a dance together, he befriended me.
Rather than compete, we did some dances
together.

A POLITICAL EDGE

Manny Diaz also got me hooked up as a volunteer on the mayor's next political campaign.

William V. Musto was reelected, and his staff took note of my abilities working with people. I was bilingual, and in Union City, with its largely Cuban population, a guy like me could be useful. I was appointed Director of Neighborhood Preservation and later became one of the few aides to the mayor.

As an employee of Union City, I used to provide government loans to homeowners so that they could beautify the city. I administered them, reviewing the applications and choosing who received the low-interest loans at three percent. I also aided the mayor with special projects and assignments, often as a go-between because I spoke Spanish.

As an aide, I helped many Cubans become United States citizens so they could vote for the mayor. Many were on the fence, thinking, *Castro's gonna go down next year. I'm not going to become a citizen here because I am a Cuban.*

I was able to persuade those people, "Hey, Castro's not going down. He has been there too many years already. If you are a U.S. citizen, you have so many rights and benefits that Cubans don't have, plus you can vote."

I helped them fill out their applications and I helped them with the test, because no one spoke English. We worked on the basics. With my dad, one of the questions I knew they would ask him was, "Who was the first president of the

United States?" To help him remember the name, I associated the answer with the George Washington Bridge, which was not too far from where he lived. When he went for his test and was asked that question, he answered, "George Washington Bridge." Thank God the examiner had some mercy and overlooked it.

I probably helped hundreds of Cubans become U.S. citizens, which was a very wonderful thing for the mayor, because he continued as mayor of Union City for about twenty-five years.

One of the dances that I promoted featured Willie Chirino, a well-known Cuban singer and a showman with his band. The mayor gave him the keys to Union City, so an article appeared in the local newspaper, *Avance,* along with a photo of me and the mayor and a few other people giving Willie the keys. I also helped Mayor Musto get elected as a state senator. Bill Musto became an influential politician until he went to prison. He was convicted for racketeering during his tenure as mayor, and I heard that he became a Christian while in prison. A couple of the Union City commissioners went to prison too.

I didn't really know anything about his racketeering. However, I didn't have strong convictions about right and wrong, either. I was aware that some of the things I did may have been illegal, but my conscience was not even pricked. I did what was right in my own eyes. I had no understanding of objective truth. Everything was judged relative to how it would benefit me, or how it would benefit someone I wanted to influence. My rule was basically, if it is OK with you and it doesn't seem to hurt me, it is OK with me too. If it hurt somebody else, that was the other person's problem, not mine.

I didn't know if it was right for me to persuade people to become U.S. citizens. I didn't really do it for their benefit. I did it for their votes, and that was selfish. My only interest in helping them pass the test was to get their vote.

I have been asked more than once, "How did your parents and some of these other people become U.S. citizens when they don't even speak English?" Basically, I coached people in such a way that they understood enough English to correctly answer the questions they'd be asked, and I did it not for their benefit, but for mine. I just used people to get what I wanted and to benefit the mayor. The mayor was my ultimate boss and the one paying me. I wanted to look good in front of him, and I liked the influence I had in the community. I was well-liked, well-respected, and acknowledged with "Eh, Manny!" when I walked down the street. Mr. Manny Mill knew everybody and they knew me. I lived for the human trinity, Me, Myself, and I. My photo in the newspaper was a regular occurrence. Anything that could help my image and my power was just fine with me. I wanted people, especially women, to become subject to me. My job, my cars, my dancing, my good looks, all of it was just a platform to chase women, and I was barely twenty years old.

Academically, I didn't do very well, which is probably no surprise. I never liked school until much later in life, when I attended Wheaton College. In high school I did so-so, and that was by the grace of God and the little discipline I could muster from my sports days. I never studied.

In college, members of the baseball team were required to have a room in the dormitory, so I had one, but I hardly ever stayed there. South Orange was about half an hour from Union City, so I slept at my parents' house when I had work to do for the mayor. I also drove back and forth a lot to promote dances, making more money on the side. After some success with that, I expanded to promoting Latin Cruises with Cuban bands and entertainers aboard the cruise.

A RISKY LIFESTYLE

I wasn't allowed to bring women into the dormitory. I never brought women to my place, anyway, and I never wanted to go home to theirs. That was my rule. I used hotels. I spent lots of money on hotels. I had a deal going with one hotel on the Hudson River in Edgewater, overlooking New York on the New Jersey side. They kept a room ready at all times. They knew I would just stop in for a few hours. Sometimes I stayed overnight, depending on the day of the week and who I brought with me. What a terrible, messed up, undisciplined way to live, and so risky.

I took a lot of risks. I was hanging by the skin of my teeth at school and should have been thrown out so many times, but I was good at manipulating my way out of trouble. I should have been on academic probation, but I would lie my way out. I was never faithful to the truth. If I had to say something that happened to be true, just to make my point, then I would tell the truth. But the truth of the statement was just coincidental; I would say whatever I needed to say to get my own way. I don't think many people recognized this about me. Maybe some of my women did, but I didn't care. They were not real people to me, just objects to be used and discarded. For me, it was all in the chase.

My mom said she noticed when I was a senior in college that I started to change. I don't think she meant for the better, either. She said the change was abrupt. As a Christian, mom reflected that perhaps God allowed me to go my own way so that He would be truly glorified when He brought me back. *Bought me back* is actually more accurate. He redeemed me with the blood of His Son, Jesus. I was very far away before that happened.

IMMEDIATE GRATIFICATION

I first saw Cecilia at my parents' house for a worship service that my mom hosted regularly after becoming a Christian. Of course, I was not interested in the service. My eyes landed on Cecilia, and I asked myself, *Man, what do I have to do to get to know this beautiful brunette?* She was a fairly new Christian at that time, and I think I corrupted her by basically faking that I had faith. I actually thought that because my middle name was Regino, after St. Regino, and I was raised in a Roman Catholic church, that made me a Christian. I had experienced baptism, first communion, and confirmation, and I attended church sometimes. That seemed sufficient to me.

I never read the Bible. I knew that my mom read her Bible all the time, so I assumed that Cecilia probably did too. I didn't let that bother me. In March of 1979 I was only one semester away from graduation, but Cecilia was a virgin goddess, and I had to have her. Driven by an impulsive nature and the need for immediate gratification, there was only one way I would get this beauty. I had to marry her first, and that meant quit school. I threw my education out the window. I was arrogant, already making a lot of money, so I figured I didn't need a college degree.

At twenty-two years old, I had no idea what a marriage commitment meant. My fidelity lasted about as long as our honeymoon. I was a terrible husband. I put Cecilia through hell. The next winter, January 14, 1980, to be exact, our son, Manny Jr., was born. While I had no clue how to be a father, I was so proud to have a son.

I worked full-time selling life insurance for Prudential, a job I got into while I was still a student at Seton Hall. I drove a Mercedes Benz 380SL by then. When I switched companies to work for Sun Life of Canada, it wasn't long before I was ready to open my own independent agency. I sold Sun Life's life policies, but I chose health and auto and other types of coverage with other companies. My office was on 48th and Bergenline Avenue in Union City. My flair for networking seemed to pay off, and I made more money than I knew how to spend. I learned pretty fast, though, and bought a Lincoln Town Coupe, an Audi 5000, and a Cadillac Seville. Nothing satisfied me anymore. It was never enough.

4

•

Salvation
AND FIRE

I N THE 1940s, the whole family hoped that Tío René would become a doctor like his grandfather. He was a very good student with a brilliant mind. His father made sure that he went to the best school available in Havana.

It so happened that a young woman took an interest in René. Apparently, his mother did not like this girl, and in a very unkind way she told her, "You take your eyes off my boy!"

When the girl's mother heard about it, she threatened my grandmother. "You are going to regret those words," she said, and because she was a *santera,* she cursed René, using witchcraft to take revenge. Demon spirits willingly cooperated, because the human motives involved were so contrary to the teachings of Christ. The whole purpose of demonic activity is to lead humanity away from the Cross. So this woman prepared a demon spirit of mental oppression and gave it specific orders to possess René and mess up his ability to think.

Within a couple of weeks, René changed dramatically. He had insomnia, and he started doing things all the wrong way. In normal conversation, his reactions were strange. He was not aggressive, not dangerous, but his perceptions threw everything off. Something was noticeably wrong.

WITCHCRAFT IN THE FAMILY

My grandmother did everything she could to find answers to the issues that plagued René. He wasn't crazy, but he was very mentally ill. The doctor gave up and said he was incurable. Mom refused to resign herself concerning her brother's hopeless agony. She consulted with many different experts, including *brujos* (witch doctors), considered the medical authorities in many Latin cultures. *Brujos* would make some kind of potion for any situation. *Curanderos,* who were like *brujos,* also had their own potions or medicines. My mom hoped to get something special to help René. Finally, he had to be put in *Hospital Siquiatrico Mazorra,* a mental hospital, and he spent twenty years there.

Until then my mom had no personal interest in *santería,* but her quest to help Tío René led to investigating witchcraft. After she became involved herself, she had the demon spirit cast out of him by a very powerful *santero* named Armando. When Tío René came out of the hospital, the years of sedation and electroshock treatment, not to mention the spiritual torture, had taken their toll. He was never the same, and he could not hold down a regular job. He managed daily functions, but not all that well. His brilliance was still evident, though, by his ability to do mental math. He made money on the streets doing *la bolita,* a form of running numbers similar to a lottery. Since gambling was illegal in Cuba, he did it without writing anything down to avoid getting caught.

Tío René tracked the names of his "customers," the people playing numbers, and banked their money. Every day they would pick their number, and they bet so many *pesos.* "Hey, René, five for tonight," Juan would say.

Tío René knew that Juan Jímenez had number five, twenty pesos. Jorge Martinez had number three, forty pesos. Guillermo had number seven, ten pesos. He kept all their bets in his head—names, numbers, and how much money they gave him—even after twenty years of being in a psychiatric ward.

My mom excelled in her spiritual practices as

a medium, using dozens of statues of Catholic saints. They were all over our house. At first glance, it looked like a Roman Catholic church. A coconut with a cigar on top was a common offering placed in front of each. In the coconut she put *agua ardiente,* which translates fire water, meaning booze. It's about 95 percent alcohol and is called white lightning in the U.S. Because Cubans were not allowed to buy alcohol, people made it at home somehow. When we came to the States, my mom continued her practices with these demonic idols.

My mom hated cigars and never smoked them unless she was in a trance, possessed by demons. I was my mom's assistant at these sessions. Two spirits in particular came often and said they were from Africa. One claimed to be female and one male. They always asked me for a cigar. Even the smell of cigars nauseated Mom any other time. She always made my dad smoke outside, but when she was active as a medium, she smoked cigars and drank the *agua ardiente.* She didn't actually drink it—she swished it in her mouth and sprayed it out all over the house. Between the smoke and the spray, our home smelled really bad.

Sometimes she would say, "Let's call a session," and she would call on the spirits. Many demons would pass through her. My part was to say, "*¡Luz y progreso!*" Light and progress! By allowing them to pass through her, Mom believed that she was assisting the spirits to work their way out of purgatory and one day be able to enter heaven. My job was to talk to the saints, and they would tell me things about my family and our future, and all that kind of stuff. Of course, I was *not* talking to the spirits of the people represented by the statues. These statues had particular demons associated with them, and the demons' names were well-known by those who practiced *santería*. I thought they were simply nicknames for the saints. I had no idea they were demons who responded when called.

Besides the many statues and offerings all over our house, candles burned all the time. Other practices used chicken blood, raw eggs, and coconuts broken outside at the four corners of the house. Mom sometimes waved seven huge handkerchiefs across a person for *despojo*, freedom from spirits. Purple, blue, yellow, red, white, brown, and green scarves were tied together, representing *Las Siete Potencias Africanas,* the Seven African Powers. Each color represented a different demon, and most *despojo* rituals employed scarf waving and screaming. *Santería* was so deceptive. Relying on demons to fulfill selfish human desires was the very cause of the rampant demonic suffering that the *santería* hoped to relieve, and any relief that came simply led to increased selfish desires.

Every Friday evening in Union City, my mom would go to the Centro de Espiritismo to help other people with their problems, like how she helped Tío René. The place was always packed, standing room only. People were hungry for help or curious about spiritual matters, but always ignorant of truth. Everyone present would have said they believed in God, or that they were Roman Catholic or Christian. They had no notion of what that really meant. Statues of the beloved saints of the church were all around the room, and that made witchcraft appear to be a good thing. Psalm 115 describes the scene very accurately.

> But their idols are silver and gold, made by the hands of men. They have mouths, but cannot speak, eyes, but they cannot see; they have ears, but cannot hear, noses, but they cannot smell; they have hands, but cannot feel, feet, but they cannot walk; nor can they utter a sound with their throats. Those who make them will be like them, and so will all who trust in them. (Psalm 115:4–8)

In other words, they were dead idols, dead gods, and anybody who trusted in them was as dead as they were. My heart was really struck when I first read Psalm 115, because this description was exactly how my parents raised me. Then I realized how much it described the way I lived here in the U.S. I had other gods that ruled over my life—my houses, my cars, my gold jewelry, my desires for women, and my money. The more I got, the more I craved more, and the worse my life became. I was about as dead as a person can get, and blind to my condition.

A TRUE SPIRITUAL AWAKENING

One of the mediums at the center became a believer in Christ, and she began to witness to my mom, who didn't really want to hear any of that. Another woman who was witnessing outside the witchcraft center told my mom, "You don't need to go back to this center anymore, because we know God. We have met the Lord, Jesus Christ." Mom had been searching earnestly for the Lord and thought she had already found Him at the center. Still, there was a hunger in her heart, so she went to church with her ex-medium friend. She heard the truth of the Gospel and responded immediately. "Jesus found me," she said, "because He is the One who searches for us. He found me when I was lost. I was found when I was so very lost in my sin."

The woman in front of the center was the pastor's wife, Lucy Sanchez, at *Iglesia de Elizabeth,* Elizabeth Church in New Jersey. After

Mom became a Christian believer, the first thing Lucy told her to do was to clean out the house. We broke all the statues to pieces. Oh, what a mess! The people at the center said Mom and all of her family would be cursed for doing such a thing. They tried to scare us. Mom was just a baby Christian, but she acted courageously and did what she knew was right in the eyes of the Lord. We got our house cleaned up, purified. I did not understand the true significance of that, but I knew that Mom had genuinely changed. Then she began to witness to me, but I would have nothing to do with Jesus.

NEW LIFE (AND DEATH)

Tío René was also a recipient of my mom's evangelistic efforts. He did not know the Lord either; Mom was the first one in our family to become a Christian. She tried to get him to come to church with her, and she continually talked to him about Christ, the Lord. She prayed earnestly for him, for me, and for everyone else she knew. Because of his mental history, René did not seem to understand when she explained the things of God. He just didn't get what she was trying to say. One day, very unexpectedly, he agreed to go to church with her, and after they came home, he said he had met the Lord. Before he went to sleep that night, he told Mom how he felt something really special, really peaceful; that he had a Bible and he was going to keep on reading. He was really looking forward to continuing his spiritual walk. He remembered going to church before, but he wanted to attend more consistently now. Then he went to sleep, and she went upstairs.

The next thing Mom knew, smoke was pouring up the stairway. "Fire, fire! Get out!" Tío René yelled up from the basement. *"¡Fuego, fuego! Salgan!"* Mom repeated to the tenants on the second floor.

Smoke billowed out the open doors, filling the air with the smell of burning wood. Lights popped on all the way down the street. In spite of the early morning hour, people crowded outside the house even before the firefighters arrived. A neighbor called my wife, Cecilia, and we came over right away. I was thankful to see Mom, Dad, and Normita unharmed. As I hugged Mom, my eyes scanned the crowd. The upstairs neighbors were out, but I could not see Tío René. Two uniformed men ran back to the truck, then down the basement steps. Another firefighter held his arms out, moving the crowd away from a water hose. I heard someone yell that the flames were doused. Yet smoke continued to escape through all available openings. Then three firefighters came out the basement door carrying something, but I could not identify what. In the beam of a fire truck's headlights, I saw them lay a black body bag into the back of a van.

Later, Mom told me she thought a cigarette might have caused the fire. Tío René left a cigarette burning, or maybe he didn't put it out completely. When he noticed the fire, Tío René managed to alert everyone else in time, but he himself did not make it out. The firefighters found him lying on the floor, near the basement door. He was not burned. We guessed that he just couldn't see the way and died of smoke inhalation.

The funeral was a couple days later. I was sad and I supposed I would miss him. My parents had taken care of Tío René all my life. His passing did not affect me deeply, though, because I was so caught up in my own affairs. I didn't care at all about Christ, so it didn't mean anything to me that Tío René became a Christian before he died. It didn't mean anything to me that God used him to save the lives of my family, or whether any of us would ever see him again.

My mom was on a campaign to win the souls of our entire family, including me. She was not a member of the Christian Secret Service. "Jesus doesn't have secret agents," she would say, and she continued to witness openly by the way she lived, the words she spoke, and the fervent prayers she prayed for all of us.

5

♦

Radical
REDEMPTION

A BUSINESS OPPORTUNITY GAVE me
the excuse I needed to escape the righteous
impact my mother tried to have on us. I opened
another insurance agency for Sun Life of Canada
in Coral Gables, Florida, and moved my family
to a suburb of Miami called Kendall. Eventually,
I gave the New Jersey office back to Sun Life
and continued to do my thing in Miami. That's
when I got into real trouble.

We were visiting my family in Union City
when my sister's boyfriend approached me with
what appeared to be a very sweet deal. I was already well-off. I didn't need the money. Nevertheless, I had become greedy and was so
self-absorbed that I never gave it a thought that
the money belonged to someone else. The deal

went like this: A woman accomplice had already stolen some blank checks from her wealthy Cuban lover. His account was worth more than $175,000. Three checks had been drafted to a bogus name and social security number, and the signatures had been forged. They just needed someone to cash the checks. With my connections in Miami, that was a no-brainer. A friend from high school worked at Coral Gables Federal Bank. I knew he would go in with us. He helped me open a checking account under that false name. I deposited the checks, waited until they cleared, then emptied the account and closed it. My cut was $50,000, and I gave the guy from New Jersey $125,000. I don't know who else was promised any of his take. That was his business. I just know that I got fifty thousand bucks for a couple hours of work. That was sweet. Each day that passed gave me more confidence to think I got away with it.

ALMOST CAUGHT

I guess that old Cuban did miss his money after all. About a month later, my secretary let me know that FBI agents had come to the office asking for me. The FBI was involved because in addition to forgery, fraud, and theft, transporting stolen property across state lines was a federal offense. When the checks were returned to the

New Jersey bank, the endorsement stamp revealed where they had been cashed. Still, I had taken precautions. I never went up to a bank teller. I was not on the cameras, and nobody could identify my face. That is, nobody but my friend the banker. I didn't expect him to rat on me, and now it was his word against mine. That didn't seem so hard to beat for an experienced manipulator like me.

The truth is, I was under the influence of the devil. The devil didn't cause it, but he did help me accomplish my own evil desires. I was deceived big time, thinking I wouldn't get caught. If I actually stopped to think about what I was doing, I might have realized that I could get caught, and then maybe I would not have done it.

I thought I was too smart to get caught, until my own stupid fingerprints were found on the checks and proved who was telling the truth. I was a dead dog if the FBI located me, so I didn't give them the opportunity. I withdrew the cash I could get to, and I told Cecilia, "We're taking a little vacation." We packed and left that same night.

Three plane tickets later, Cecilia, Manny Jr., and I were on our way to San Juan, Puerto Rico, where we applied for our U.S. passports. Because of my connections, we were able to get a personal favor and we all received our passports the next day. Manny Jr. was about four years old, and Cecilia was seven months pregnant with our second child. However, we couldn't stay there long because Puerto Rico was a U.S. territory and I could still be arrested. I had to tell Cecilia the truth and she was furious with me for deceiving her. I was so terrible to her.

We tried the Dominican Republic for about six days, but I didn't like it there. The country was too small, so we moved on. I had no plan. I wasn't thinking clearly. I thought I was a tough guy, but honestly, I was scared to death and desperately running as far away as I could get. We landed in Bogotá, Colombia. I lasted one night in the high altitude with difficulty breathing. Next, we tried Medellín, Colombia. Poor Cecilia. I made her do all this traveling when she was so pregnant.

I didn't like Medellín, either, and I felt Colombia was altogether too much of a risk, too close to the U.S. I considered going back to Spain, and then thought of Brazil, but I didn't know any Portuguese. Finally, I settled on Venezuela. Somebody told me there was a large Cuban community in Caracas, about 100,000 people, so I thought, *Oh, man, let's go there!*

THE CUBAN IN VENEZUELA

In the first month, I opened a small Cuban cafeteria, El Rincón de La Habana. After two more months, I moved two doors down to expand the cafeteria and opened a restaurant right upstairs, which took some underhanded scheming and some money. I knew how to work fast, like my dad, and found investors and a Venezuelan partner. In no time we had the best Cuban restaurant in Venezuela. It was a luxurious establishment, complete with maître d' captains and a gourmet chef. I was there, dressed up in my suit, being Mr. Big Shot Cuban guy, and I still had some hair. I used the restaurant and its glamour just to get women. I was the owner and I did as I pleased, working the room, especially during happy hour. Cuban men were very popular with Venezuelan women.

I left home at six o'clock in the morning and returned around midnight, just like my dad. I walked from our apartment to the restaurant. I didn't have a car and didn't need one. A local taxi driver became my personal chauffeur. He ate well in my restaurant, and when I wanted to go somewhere, he took me. Anywhere I wanted. I was amazed at how much power I had.

Currency in Venezuela is named after a national hero, Simón Bolívar. When we arrived in Venezuela, seventy bolivars was equivalent to one U.S. dollar. Anyone with dollars had a lot of power, so it wasn't that amazing that when I snapped my fingers things happened. Everyone knew me as *El Cubano,* The Cuban.

When the time came for my wife to deliver our child, she called me at the restaurant. I was too absorbed in my own world, so I sent my personal taxi to make sure she got to the hospital immediately. How insensitive. I should have taken her there myself. I finally arrived a couple hours later. In my heart, I was thrilled to be having another child, but my behavior gave no indication of how I felt. And I hid behind the long hours, rationalizing that working hard made me a good husband and father. Yet, no amount of money, prestige, and power would ever make up for my absence at such a significant time. By God's grace, on November 7, 1984, our beautiful little daughter, Cesia, was born.

THE DANGERS OF LIFE ON THE EDGE

Early one morning on my way to work I got robbed. Two guys with guns, pointing them in my face, got my money, my passport, everything. I gave it all to them. They didn't kill me, thank God. My mom must have been praying for me, and God protected me that day.

That wasn't the first time I escaped with my life. During my Latin Cruise days I partnered with a couple other guys I really didn't know very well. Some very intimidating men visited me in my hotel room. It turned out that my partners were involved with loan sharks and owed these men money. Their pistols were demanding payment. The same poor judgment that got me those partners emerged again when I actually told those thugs, "I don't owe you anything. They owe you. I don't, so get out of here." They didn't shoot. They left.

I found out later that loan sharks charged 100 percent interest and had no qualms about killing defaulters. I could have been dead so many times. I always spent more money than I had, I was always in over my head, and I was always involved in too many things at one time.

Another time in Union City, my choice for the night told me she was single. I broke my number one rule and went back to her place. Really she was only separated. At three o'clock in the morning her estranged husband was banging on the door with a gun. Cuban husbands are insanely jealous. I thought, *Oh, man, now I'm in for it.* It was a very uncomfortable fight for me. I whacked the gun away easily using judo. But I was half asleep and completely undressed. He had a hard time getting hold of me with no clothes to grab at, but he managed to pick up the gun somehow. I pushed his hand back, but the handle hit me right in the forehead. Anyone with young children would know that even superficial head wounds bleed profusely, but when he saw all that blood, he just ran, and I didn't follow him. I got dressed and dragged myself to the hospital, bleeding all over the place and disgusted with the mess. God protected me again.

CAUGHT BY GRACE

We lived in Caracas almost two years while I was on the run. One day the FBI paid a visit to my dad. One of the agents was Puerto Rican, so he explained in Spanish what I had done. That night my dad telephoned me with my mom on the extension. My dad said, "Manolito, I know what you have done. The FBI came to see me at the meat store. I know you are facing fifty-five years behind bars. Let me ask you a question. If I died tonight, could you come to my funeral?" I was silent.

I broke down and cried. I couldn't answer when he asked me that question. I just began to weep from deep inside my soul. Then my mom began to speak, reminding me that I had sinned against a holy God. She pleaded with me to repent of my sins. "To repent is to live," she said, and told me I needed to trust in Jesus Christ and make Him Lord and Savior of my life. "You need forgiveness for your sins, Manny, and He will do that now if you ask Him." And then she just started praying right over the telephone, "Oh, God, save my son. Make him see how lost he is, how far he is from You. He's on his way to hell, God. He needs You. Help him see he cannot run from You. Father, You promised to forgive. I pray my son will ask Your forgiveness and follow Jesus."

I was not a person who cried, ever, but I could not help myself. I was sobbing. The Holy Spirit quickened my spirit and opened the eyes of my heart to see what I could not see before (Ephesians 1:18). I prayed right out loud like my mom, "Oh, God, please forgive me for all I have done. I have sinned against You, God. I'm guilty and I'm ashamed. I don't want to run anymore, Lord. Save me. Come into my heart and change my life. God, I need Your help. Give me the courage to face what I've done and make it right. Give me the courage to face my family and the world with the truth."

I could hear the joy in my mom's voice. She was praising God and thanking Him for what He had done. I felt like the whole world was lifted off my back, until my mom asked me, "When are you coming back?" I answered that coming back was not part of the deal.

"You must come back and face the music. You must surrender to the FBI and do what is right." Yes, I had prayed for courage and a way to make things right, but surrender was not what I had in mind!

"Manolito, God promises He will never leave us or forsake us. Remember that. Hebrews chapter 13, verse 5. You invited Jesus into your heart, and He will be with you from now on. Even if you have to go to prison."

I knew, when that river of tears came out like an avalanche, it was a total surrender to the true God of the universe, to His Son Jesus. I knew that something radical had taken place in my heart. My mind was set now, and there was no going back. I held on to the truth of that one verse, Hebrews 13:5, which became my life verse. The Holy Spirit of God dwelt in my heart now, and I would never, ever again be alone. It was like the gates of heaven opened up so wide and I saw God sitting on His throne. I saw His majestic power and I knew I had been cleansed. Jesus' blood made that difference. His blood was so fresh, and He washed me in that blood. I came out on the other side with a new perspective that I never had before. I knew what I had to do, and it was radical. Two weeks later, my dad booked me and my family on a Pan American flight headed to New York City.

What I did not realize at the time was that my dad became a Christian on the telephone right along with me on January 28, 1986. He had seen the huge change in my mom's way of life, but up until that day, he was not a believer. I didn't have much opportunity to get to know the new Manolo, a man of God. I went to prison, then went to school and settled in the

Midwest, so the distance kept us apart. We talked on the phone, and had brief visits whenever I could get back east. In the latter years of his life he became a faithful Christian.

6

•

Complicated
CONSEQUENCES

JUST LIKE NICODEMUS in John 3, my dad and I were both born again. The Holy Spirit gave me the courage I needed to come home and take responsibility for the crimes I committed. In February of 1986, Cecilia, Manny Jr., and Cesia flew with me to New York City, where I surrendered to the FBI at Kennedy International Airport. When we deplaned from Venezuela, FBI agents were waiting. My wife and children were escorted away by a female agent, and the others took me into a private room where they cuffed my hands right away. They were kind not to do that in front of my family. My dad was the one who arranged my surrender with the FBI, so they showed respect to my dad as well by not humiliating the whole family in public. Although I came back voluntarily, transport to and from the car required handcuffs. We rode pretty much in silence to the Regional Office in Newark, New Jersey, where FBI agents booked and fingerprinted me, confiscated my U.S. passport, and let me out on bond.

My wife and children went home with her parents to their home in Harrison, New Jersey. Later that week, we rented a basement apartment near both our families and I managed a Burger King for three months, awaiting sentencing. (I pled guilty, so there was no need for a trial.) I heard that my sister's boyfriend was convicted and went to prison, as was the woman who stole the checks and the person who forged them. I never met either of those two. The bank employee was cleared when he gave the FBI my name. Because I pled guilty, and by God's mercy, the judge sentenced me to only three years at Allenwood Federal Prison in Montgomery, Pennsylvania.

Typically, incarceration begins immediately after sentencing, but I did not go to prison right away. The judge allowed me to go home for three more months and report to prison on my own, unescorted. That was grace.

INTO PRISON

When the time came, my family drove with me to prison. We pulled into the prison parking lot just before noon, at the peak of a beautiful day, July 15, 1986. The summer sun was high in the sky, bright and hot, but to me it was a terrible day. I walked up to the gate and reported my name. It was not a very intimidating gate, just a door with a couple of correctional officers standing nearby. Nevertheless, I was scared and my family was too. The visiting room was right next to the gate. Images of the painted brick walls, light-brownish chairs, and vending machines burned into my memory right then. That was where my family waited while I met with my case manager and my counselor. A correctional officer came to take me away. Tears flowed freely as I hugged Cecilia, hugged my dad and mom, and hugged my children goodbye. Leaving them was very hard for me, and the future was so uncertain. All of us put everything in God's hands.

Allenwood Federal Prison is a camp, not like a maximum-security prison with barbed wire and razor ribbon. There was no fence at all around the property, but because of this, procedures were more strict inside. Inmates were counted seven times a day, with different counts throughout the twenty-four-hour cycle. At certain counts, we had to stand at attention.

After I changed into prison clothes, I was fingerprinted again and checked in, and given an ID card with my number, 07592-050. Humiliating does not begin to describe the experience. I had boots that didn't fit, pants that didn't fit, and for the first two weeks, I had no pillow. My top bunk, a small bed, was in a dormitory with seventy-four other men, so it was a huge change from the lifestyle I was used to living. I felt terrible about the circumstances, but God was faithful to me, just like the Scripture in Hebrews 13 said, from day one.

Before prison, I had never made a bed in my life. I never cleaned my room. I never did anything remotely like that. During the first six weeks, my work assignment was to clean bathrooms. What a wonderful, humbling experience that was, but it got me a promotion to work at UNICOR, the Federal Prison System Industry. Working in the office as a bookkeeper, I made forty-four cents an hour. Eventually, I worked my way up to $1.10 an hour plus ten cents an hour for seniority. From 7:00 to 3:30 each day, I made $1.20 per hour, and I got to know my boss, Mr. Martello, pretty well. He was not a Christian, but he began to look at me differently. "You know, this guy is for real!"

A DIRTY JOB AND A LESSON OR TWO

Bob Brantley and Jim Williams were the first inmates who befriended me. We laughed a lot as I described my first attempts to clean a toilet. A correctional officer brought me into a bathroom and said, "This is your duty, to clean all the bathrooms and toilets in UNICOR." What a filthy mess! Being a Christian now, I aimed to have the best-cleaned bathrooms in the whole prison. I was beginning to get a glimpse of God's holiness, and I wanted God to be pleased with me. Although I didn't fully understand, it seemed to me that my actions had to connect some way to how I felt about God. He deserved my best effort.

True, I didn't know how to clean a bathroom, but I knew what a clean one was supposed to look like. I traveled in high-class circles where the bathrooms were always spotlessly clean, and at least I knew the difference between an unappealing bathroom and a clean one. So I set my expectations accordingly. Using whatever supplies they gave me, I gave it my best shot. The first step was the hardest. I knew I had to put my hand in the bowl to get it clean, so I had to go deep! That was one way God prepared me for a ministry of "getting dirty," getting involved in an up-close-and-personal way with other people.

Cleaning bathrooms was where I first began to think about work ethics and principles like "hitting the corners." To look superficially clean wasn't good enough, because I wanted the bathroom to *be* clean; so I went underneath, around the bottom, and down the back of each fixture.

Probably right after I finished, some other guy came and messed it up again. Nevertheless, that was my job eight hours a day, all day long cleaning the bathrooms and maintaining them.

God ordained this work for me, because I was too proud, too full of Manny Mill. Cleaning toilets was a good beginning. I began to sense that my salvation was for real, because this physical, repetitive, and sometimes unpleasant work didn't produce a complaining attitude, not even hidden in my heart. Compared to the old Manny Mill, this was a striking change. The way I used to feel was gone. I didn't feel that way anymore, and I knew that I had nothing to do with the change. That is an important point. It had to have been an outside force. It had to have been the Lord Jesus, through the working of the Holy Spirit. I recognized this as more proof that my day of redemption was for real!

LEARNING THAT GOD IS REAL

As I grew and developed into a different person, I knew one thing—I did not want to go back to the way I was. As I looked back on the man I used to be, I didn't like anything I saw. The closer I got to Jesus, the better I was going to be. It was a tremendously important discovery for me that I could not help myself. I had nothing to bring to the table. God was doing it all. My task was to learn to submit, surrender, and let God have His way, but sometimes I failed miserably, because my stubborn, sinful human nature resisted change.

Of course, I did not know God very well, but I knew that He was for real and that authenticity attracted me. God the Almighty, the One that Christ represented and revealed, drew me to Himself like a magnet. The more I read the Bible and the more I understood, the more my passion to please God grew. I didn't know much about passion for His glory or passion for His joy. That came later. I just wanted to be for real and not have to fake it anymore. I knew who I had become, and I wanted that to show.

One night, I was gathering guys in the dormitory for a prayer meeting when a tall, skinny, blond-haired, angry inmate confronted me. Honestly, I didn't know what was up, except this guy didn't like me very much and didn't need an excuse to get in my face. I foolishly asked him, "What's your problem, man?"

He pointed his finger into my chest, accenting every syllable as he rudely spoke, "My problem is you!" My eyes bounced down to his finger and up into his face, and then down at his finger again. I remember thinking that his long mustache and wire-rimmed glasses really accentuated his frown. What an unhappy guy he was. God gave me a tremendous sense of self-control. The old Manny Mill would have reacted and let him have it, which would have landed me right in the hole. What a lousy witness that would have been for the church. That was a test of self-control for me, but even more a test of trust. I had not yet learned to think ahead about the consequences of my actions. The Holy Spirit simply made it possible for me to be restrained rather than retaliate. Three days later, that guy was transferred out of the prison.

A GROWING PRISON CHURCH

I craved understanding, so I had a Spanish Bible and an English Bible that I read side by side, a section in one and then in the other. The chaplain at Allenwood was not particularly in-terested in the Bible, nor did he manifest his relationship with Jesus in ways that helped me understand anything. He used a special book for the worship services, not a Bible. Everything was by that little book from his denomination.

Only twelve men were attending church then. A couple of them were really on-fire Chris-tian believers, so they embraced me and we de-cided to pray together about the chaplain. That's when my passion for prayer began, and every time I prayed, God responded. Not that He al-ways did what I asked or expected. I just be-lieved God when He said to ask. God removed this chaplain from the prison, and for two and one-half months we had no chaplain. As a baby Christian, God allowed me to be a surrogate chaplain to others, and the church began to grow. Three of us began a Tuesday night Spanish service that grew to seventy men. Different prayer groups met with fifty or more men in each group, morning, afternoon, and evening. I led these prayer groups each day.

When our new chaplain, Manny Cordero, arrived, he was a blessing to everyone, but especially to me. He and I became close, and together we began to get the church body organized. The prison church appointed elders and deacons and began to have regular meetings to address the needs of church members. Inmates became involved in organizing services, like setting the order of service, and I became head of the in-prison elder board. I began to realize that the church, the body of Christ, was real, and probably just as real outside prison as it was in Allenwood Federal Prison Camp.

FAMILY VISITS

A month and a half went by before my family came back for a visit. The prison administration allowed us to have contact visits. In jails or in a super-max facility, they restricted contact, and visits were through glass windows with telephones. I was glad that we did not have to deal with those glass stalls. We were so glad to see each other, but it was hard, with a capital H. "Why don't you come home with us, Daddy?" Manny Jr. pleaded. Oh, man, hearing that hurt, and I wept big time. We paid the Jaycees a couple of dollars and they took a Polaroid picture of all of us in the visiting room.

The ride from Union City, New Jersey, to Montgomery, Pennsylvania, was about four hours, which limited our visits to even less than the prison quota per inmate. My dad took off work to drive Cecilia and my kids to Allenwood. Mom and Normita came along, too, and helped Cecilia, because traveling with small children was always difficult.

Cecilia was a strong woman and she wanted everything to work out, but circumstances made it tough on her. When we left Venezuela, we lost everything, leaving it all behind, clinging to the fact that we still had each other. After my incarceration began, reality hit her hard. I was not there for her, and I had never been there for her, really. Ten months into my sentence, we planned to have a new start. Cecilia promised to come for a weekend marriage seminar sponsored by Prison Fellowship. Manny Cordero and I planned the event, and I organized many of the details. We were at the door welcoming all the wives, and everybody came in smiling, but Cecilia never showed up. Finally Chaplain said, "Well, Manny, we have to go to the Stone Chapel."

"But Cecilia is not here," I pleaded.

"Let me call," Chaplain declared, trying to sound hopeful. He called Cecilia's home, but no one answered.

"OK. Can we call her mother?" So he did, and her mother told him, flatly, "She moved. She moved to Miami." She would not tell him anything else.

That felt like a bucket of cold water dumped on my head. I could not abandon my responsibilities, but I sure didn't feel like being at the marriage seminar without her. That was another test to develop my character.

A few weeks after the seminar, divorce papers came. I never blamed Cecilia for that. I blamed myself. As I grew in the Lord, I realized more and more how much damage I did to her, and to my parents, and to my children. But God, in His mercy, gave me a new beginning.

GOD'S CLASSROOM

Like the story of Joseph in Genesis 39–41, God used imprisonment to prepare me for future leadership. Not that I was anything like the great leader Joseph, but we both received basic training in prison. God gave me a desire to get into His Word. I had no theological schooling, not even Sunday school experiences, but I had lots of time, holy determination, and the influence of the Christian volunteers who came to worship with us in prison. Chaplain knew how to choose volunteers who were committed and solid in their biblical teaching. Some were charismatic and some were Pentecostal. Their influence stayed with me, even as my theology stretched beyond those experiences.

God also gave me a compelling desire to work with all types of people and taught me the need to be submissive to others, because of my tendency to be a lone ranger. I was impulsive, quick to make decisions without consulting anyone, and comfortable with the philosophy "my way or the highway." That was not God's way, and Chaplain Cordero had to get in my face. Often, after talking with him, I left his office crying and angry. I wrote long notes and tucked them under his door, relentlessly hunting him down, always to defend why I should get my own way. I gave him just cause to get in my face repeatedly.

Puerto Ricans and Cubans typically didn't get along, but this Puerto Rican chaplain did not let that stop him from loving an overzealous Cuban inmate like me. He saw potential in me and encouraged the development of ministry skills. He attended the Spanish service on Tuesdays, but allowed me to preach. Sunday mornings, he led the service, and he always gave me a part. Sometimes I prayed or helped with the music, not singing or anything like that, just scheduling who would do it, because I was not very musical. However, in the Spanish service I sang right along with everybody else, because the congregation was large enough to drown me out.

Another attempt to stretch my abilities came when Chaplain Cordero recommended that I attend a Discipleship Seminar sponsored by Prison Fellowship Ministries (PFM). They held these seminars in Reston, Virginia, so after Prison Fellowship approved my participation, I had to get clearance to leave the prison. Both my case manager and my counselor insisted, "No way. Manny Mill cannot go." I was too high-risk as a former fugitive from the FBI. Chaplain fought for me with everything he had, but they still said no. He was even more persistent than I was. He so much wanted me to have this experience and training. We prayed, asking God to do something about the situation, although I had no idea what He could do. Not long after we committed to pray regularly about it, the counselor and the case manager were transferred out of the prison and replaced by new people.

Chaplain had the audacity to go back and present the opportunity to the new staff. They agreed to process the request, but even with their cooperation, it seemed impossible that the paperwork would come back from the Bureau of Prisons in time for me to make the seminar scheduled to take place in Reston, Virginia, near Washington, D.C. Chaplain Cordero persevered in prayer and, miraculously, everything needed came back in time. God opened the gates for me to leave prison for two weeks. Gordon Barnes, a Prison Fellowship volunteer, drove me and another man from Allenwood to the airport. As we talked in the car, I realized that my faith had been strengthened by the way God changed the circumstances. God had His hand on me, but I had no idea why. The thirteen days in Washington were significantly blessed. Attending that seminar changed the course of my young Christian life.

7

•

Extraordinary
DISCIPLESHIP

WHY DID GOD GIVE me favor with Ken
Wessner, a successful businessman with a
full schedule, when I was a prisoner serving time
for a felony? I have no idea. Ken was not lacking
people in his life. A man of his stature had personal friends like Chuck Colson and Billy Graham, and more than enough to do in a day. Yet,
by the sovereignty of God and His providential
power, Ken and Norma Wessner found the time
to make me part of their lives and their family.

For nearly two weeks I was at Prison Fellowship's Discipleship Seminar, learning from Bible
teachers and experiencing Christian fellowship
in a setting other than prison. It was an exciting
time of being equipped for ministry.

We were paired off and lodged in cottages
where we slept and ate our breakfast. Classroom

discipleship was held each morning at Prison Fellowship Ministries' headquarters in Reston, Virginia. After lunch, we had other scheduled activities, like speaking to various groups or meeting government leaders. Over the two weeks we met with several church groups, including youth groups, the NAACP, the Presidential Prayer Breakfast, congressmen, senators, and Michael Quinlan, the director of the Bureau of Prisons at that time. I also met, had lunch with, and got to know the former governor of Minnesota, The Honorable Al Quie, who serves on the Prison Fellowship Board of Trustees.

In between studying and ministering, we were privileged to tour Washington, D.C., itself as well as the PFM headquarters, and we ate out at a couple of soul food restaurants. The idea was to give people positive exposure to ex-prisoners, and to give us opportunity to practice the leadership skills we were learning in discipleship class, in the hope that this would equip us to go back into prison and disciple others. The two-week experience culminated with a PFM dinner at the Washington Hilton the night before we were to return to prison.

A PROVIDENTIAL MEETING

The guest speaker at the dinner was Billy Graham, and somewhere between four and five hundred people attended, including key PFM donors. The only people I knew were the six men I had just met over the last two weeks, and we were directed to sit at different tables around the room. By the providence of God, I sat next to Ken Wessner. Not just at the same table, but right next to the man. He was a member of Prison Fellowship's executive board, so he knew that inmates were coming to the dinner. He had no choice but to say something to me.

He was very calm and looked celebrated in his dark suit. He glanced at my name tag and said, "Well, Manny, I hear that you are going back to prison tomorrow. I know that you have been here for several days, attending the Washington Discipleship Seminar. Have you thought about what you are going to do when you get out of prison?"

I responded, "Sir, by faith," with my distinctively charismatic language, "by faith, I am going to Wheaton *Bible* College, because I want to study the Bible." I had never heard of any Christian colleges before. I was a rookie Christian, excited for Jesus, and just beginning to get a taste of the joy that comes from being used by God. Several weeks before the seminar, Chaplain Cordero found out about the Charles W. Colson Scholarship for Ex-Offenders and requested all the application paperwork for me. I immediately filled out every page and mailed it back to the college.

Mr. Wessner looked at me kind of puzzled, and in a very nice way corrected me. He said, "Manny, I think the name of that school is not Wheaton *Bible* College. It is just Wheaton College."

So, of course, in my naive excitement, not knowing who this man was, I wanted to make my point. "Sir, by faith, I am going to Wheaton *Bible* College, and I know this, because I just applied for a scholarship there!"

"Wow, you did?" he replied, genuinely interested in that fact. We went head to head a couple more times, and finally he had to put his foot down, being the leader that he was. He said, "Manny, my name is Kenneth Wessner, and I am the Chairman of the Board of Wheaton College." Oh! I wanted to crawl under the table and hide.

I didn't know what to say, so I just humbled myself and acknowledged the obvious, "Yes, sir. You are right." During the rest of our conversation, he gave me some helpful information about Wheaton College.

On other occasions, Ken fondly retold the story of how we met, and referred to it as the clincher of our relationship. It somehow endeared me to him, and certainly left an impression on both of us. He being up high in life and me being down low, the fact that he was willing to come to my level was a huge inspiration to me.

Ken wrote to me while I was still in prison. I will never forget that, and I saved all his letters. Not only was he the chairman of the Wheaton College Board of Trustees, but he was also Chairman of the Board of ServiceMaster Corporation. Both positions demanded a lot of time and effort. Yet he took time to write and encourage me.

THE LAST MONTHS INSIDE

Several Prison Fellowship volunteers ministered to me while I was in prison, some who came regularly to Allenwood and some, like Roy Prescott, whom I just met at the Discipleship Seminar. The outside contacts that God provided for me kept me from sinking into the depths of a desolate, disconnected, distorted life inside prison. Like the apostle Paul, I was convinced that nothing separated me from the love of God in Christ Jesus (Romans 8:38–39). His constant presence was real to me, but something happened when I experienced God's love through the flesh of other believers. My faith was strengthened and my hope burned brighter. I served my time more productively, because there was more to my life than just marking off the days until my release. Letters from Christians ministered to me in important ways, but the visits made an exceptionally powerful impact.

My release from prison was serendipitous. I applied for the scholarship at Wheaton by faith because the admission date was August of 1988. I was not supposed to be released until I served 85 percent of my sentence, which would have been January of 1989. Even with all the possible adjustments I was aware of, I figured the minimum I would have to serve was twenty-four months. I trusted in God, that if He wanted me to go to Wheaton College, He would work it out. Completing the application was the easy part. Waiting on God was more difficult. Much to my surprise, God released me April 6, 1988, exactly two months after I met Ken Wessner.

A GROWING RELATIONSHIP

Many people think that Ken Wessner had an affluent upbringing, but he did not. He grew up during the Depression and, along with the rest of the country, experienced its humble circumstances. He knew what it meant to have nothing, yet he became a "Who's Who" in the business world.

His son-in-law Ross told me that Ken believed in investing in others because of what others' encouragement had meant in his own life. Ken was excited about me, because he saw how I had been transformed by God, and he wanted to see me have the opportunity for the scholarship.

Talk about taking a chance—he loved me without really knowing me. He went to bat for me with the scholarship committee and championed my cause. He also put the fear of God in me like no one else could. When I first arrived at Wheaton, Ken ate with me in the student dining hall. He looked me right in the eyes, pointed his finger close to my nose, and said, "Manny, you have no room to fail. You have no choice but to make it." Those words have rung continually in my ears ever since.

Ken was so much like a father to me. The first time I went to see him at ServiceMaster, he personally gave me a tour of the whole place. People saw me walking with him, and, of course, when the boss walked by, people stopped and greeted him. He introduced me to hundreds of people on our little tour through ServiceMaster. Ken treated me with dignity and respect, and not as an ex-convict, second-class citizen.

He also loved baseball. He was a lefty, and a pitcher. Things in common added to the fact that we really connected well, but I always held a high respect for him. He insisted that I stop calling him Mr. Wessner, and he told me, "You either call me Ken or Wes. If not, I am going to have to start calling you Señor Mill." Long before I was comfortable with it, I chose to call him Ken.

Ken was so proud when I received my bachelor's degree. He was on the platform, because he also received a degree that day, an honorary doctorate, so his family came to celebrate and I met them for the first time. Ken said he wished he had been the one to sign my diploma, but he was no longer Chairman of the Board. His good friend Bud Knoedler was now the chairman, also sitting on the platform near Ken, and the one who signed my diploma. Ken said since he couldn't sign my diploma, he was glad that it was Bud who did.

During graduate school, in collaboration with several others I began to develop the whole concept of a Koinonia House, a family home where prisoners could live after their release that would help integrate them back into society and let them see a healthy family life. Ken was behind the idea right away. He wanted his family to share in that vision, so when we finally got a house, he invited his children to come over to see it. Ken and Norma donated furniture and spent time at the house, excited to have seen the seeds of a ministry develop into a whole discipleship concept. We were living with the first of many Christian ex-prisoners, and Ken was overjoyed to share the experience with us.

One day I called him and said, "I really need to talk to you."

"Tomorrow," he said.

"OK, what time?" We met at 6:00 A.M. at a McDonald's. He made time for me. He always looked out for my best interests, just like a good friend would.

When Manny Jr. lost his home in Florida due to Hurricane Andrew, he called to ask, "Can I come and live with you, Daddy?"

"When?" I replied, knowing we had no money for a plane ticket or anything else that he desperately needed.

"How about tomorrow, Daddy?"

I did not personally tell Ken. Somehow Ken found out about it, and he took care of everything. God knows that I never asked Ken for money. I didn't have to, because he was generous to us and demonstrated his love for us. Even on his deathbed, he wanted to bless me, Manny Mill. I received a call from his son, David, asking me to speak at the memorial service when the Lord called Ken home. Family was an important part of life for Ken and Norma, and so the close relationship that started between me and Ken carried over with his wife and children in the years that followed Ken's death. His influence in my life has been profound, to the point that many of the people I know and love today are relationships that came through Ken and Norma.

8

•

Federal
PAROLE

M OM AND DAD WERE waiting at the gate on April 6, 1988, when I walked out of prison. They took me home to New Jersey for a couple of weeks while plans took shape for a move to Illinois. I was free at last! Yet I had much to learn about living as a Christian outside of prison and handling freedom responsibly.

One of the first persons I called from my parents' house was Ken Wessner. I held his business card in my sweaty hand, informed him of my early release, and told him I wanted to go to Wheaton College. The conversation was short. Three weeks later I was on my way to be interviewed as a candidate for the Charles W. Colson Scholarship.

I also called Chuck Colson's office to let

him know that I had been released. His assistant called back a few days later to tell me he would be sending a photo that Chuck had signed for me. It was a group shot of all the guys from the Discipleship Seminar with Chuck Colson and Billy Graham, taken that night at the Hilton. Then Colson's assistant mentioned that Chuck would soon be speaking at a Prison Fellowship fund-raiser at the Marriott in Newark, New Jersey. I went to hear Chuck, and he seemed very happy to see me. We talked and he prayed for me, especially about the upcoming interview in Wheaton.

Roy Prescott had introduced himself to me at the Washington Hilton and later visited me in prison. He had only known me three months, yet he demonstrated love for me tangibly by providing my airline ticket from Newark to Chicago.

WHEATON COLLEGE

On May 1, 1988, I arrived in Wheaton. I had never been to Chicago and had no clue where Wheaton was, let alone what the culture would be like. Everything was a complete surprise to me, and I soon realized that the feeling was mutual. The people of Wheaton were in for a shock as well.

Rob Ribbe, a student and an intern with the Institute for Prison Ministries, picked me up at the airport and took me to the Billy Graham Center on the campus of Wheaton College. Interviews were already scheduled with several key people who assessed my suitability to receive a Colson Scholarship. Included on the list were two professors from the Sociology/Anthropology Department, Dr. Ivan Faas and Dr. Alvaro Nieves. In the student development department, I interviewed with Dr. Henry Nelson, but it was Rodney Sisco who took me all over campus and helped me get settled in Wheaton. I had no place to stay for two days, so they put me in Fischer Hall, which was the building farthest away from the Institute for Prison Ministries. Was that a hint about my loud speaking volume?

Hutz Hertzberg was chaplain at the college then. We first met when Hutz was walking west on the sidewalk between the Memorial Student Center and Blanchard Hall. Rodney and I came from the other direction, and when we got within earshot of each other, Rodney called out, "Chaplain Hutz, I would like to introduce you to a new student here."

Hutz barely got his hand stuck out to shake mine, and before he could say anything, he heard my thick Cuban accent blurting out, "Hello, my name is Manny Mill and I'm on fire for Jesus! *¡Aleluya!*"

Hutz just shook his head. He later told me his thoughts went something like, *This poor guy—I see he's an older student—this poor guy is never gonna make it here. He thinks this is like a summer camp or something.* Hutz was glad to be proven wrong about me. He was also wrong about "summer camp." One condition of my acceptance as a Colson Scholar was that I complete a summer course, their High Road program at Honey Rock Camp, and it was no summer camp, believe me. I was enrolled for the July session.

In the meantime, from May until July, I lived in Crystal Lake, Illinois. Diann Barnes, the wife of my friend Gordon in Pennsylvania, had a brother, David Cozad, who was the pastor of Christian Fellowship of Crystal Lake. Gordon called David and told him about my situation. David and Diann had another brother, Donald, who was incarcerated. That made David more willing to get involved, but he still had questions to be addressed and reservations about welcoming a Cuban ex-prisoner into their fellowship. Final arrangements were made, and the associate pastor, David Masey, drove me from the Billy Graham Center to the place that would be home for the next two months.

MAMA LIBBY

Mama Libby Bland lived with her son, Ken, who had his own painting and drywall business.

She was retired and able to be home during the day, and she opened up her home to me. She let me help her around the house, since I had no money to pay for living there. I cleaned the house, helped in the kitchen, and did their yard work. Making myself available gave me dignity. "What can I do to help you, Mama?" I often asked, and she would think up something. Mama Libby encouraged me, and she appreciated my drive to perform with excellence, regardless of the task. I was such a baby Christian believer, just out of prison a few weeks, and she understood how needy I was. Sometimes we just talked. She listened mostly, patiently letting me get a lot of things off my chest. From my first day out, I wanted to be for real. That was so important to me, and Mama Libby seemed to understand, which was the comfort I needed.

Animals were of no interest to me, and the cat, *el gato,* that lived with Mama Libby sensed this. We mutually respected a healthy distance from each other, until one evening when I was cleaning a window in my room. It was past sundown, and the evening air from the open window beckoned *el gato.* He must have seriously weighed the pros and cons of an escape that required trespassing through my room. When he made his move, *el gato* was out that window even before I had time to realize he was in the vicinity. Man, I didn't like that cat, but he was important to Ken, so that made him important to me. We spent the next hour searching the neighborhood to find him. Ken finally found *el gato* sitting in the bushes next to the window, pleased with the fuss he stirred up, I'm certain.

The whole church in Crystal Lake embraced me and became a home church that stuck by me and supported me through trials much more serious than *el gato*. Their example was the basis for the postprison ministry that the Holy Spirit was beginning to reveal to me.

HIGH ROAD

The peaceful days with Mama Libby ended abruptly. In no way was I prepared for what followed—High Road, in the beautiful north woods of Three Lakes, Wisconsin, off the coast of Lake Superior. I was told that High Road would be a great experience for me, that I would be in the wilderness, like Moses, fasting and praying and really getting myself equipped for the challenges of college. I thought that meant a nice, quiet, reflective retreat time in the secluded surroundings of nature.

Every day presented new challenges and obstacles to be overcome, especially rappelling and climbing. Ken Kaelish was one of our leaders in the wilderness. When we came to the side of a mountain one morning, I said to him, "I am not going down. I have never done this before and I am not going to do it now." In light of all the risky, crazy things I had already done in my life, I'm not sure what my problem was exactly.

"Well, if you don't go down, we're not leaving," Ken said, causing me to think about the meaning of teamwork. "When you go, we go." By God's grace, we all made it down the mountain.

My fingers and toes were covered with blisters. Drought hit that summer and I was always desperate for water. Finding that I was allergic to evergreen trees only added to my misery. Yet meeting Jim Hoek made it all worth it. God sent him to High Road just to bless me, because he didn't even know why he wanted to do the program. His wife, Bea, didn't know and his son, Jon, didn't know either. Jim never went to Wheaton College. He was older than I, but he just felt it was an experience that he wanted. What timing. During the trip, he lost his spoon, so we shared mine for a while. Bea said she knew he was in trouble, because in spite of all the stamped envelopes and paper she sent with him, the only letter he wrote said, "Dear Bea, Please pray. Love, Jim." We became good friends, and we continued to have many interesting experiences together, especially when we ministered together at Danville Correctional Center in Danville, Illinois.

On the final day of High Road, the whole

group loaded a van and headed back to Honey Rock Camp. We thought we were finished until the van stopped and our leaders booted us out into the wilderness again.

"What happened?" I said in a rather concerned tone.

"Run to the camp," were the horrifying words I heard coming from inside the van.

"Run where?" I asked, truly panicked. "How am I going to get there? I have no idea where I am!"

"Find your way there," were the last words I heard as the van drove away. Tired, exhausted really, and lost, the five of us figured it out together, and ran the eight miles to get to the finish line back at the camp. That was a valuable lesson in teamwork, perseverance, and how to press on and finish the course.

The first term paper I wrote as a student at Wheaton College was a comparison between my experience of High Road and prison. I concluded that prison was better than High Road.

Dr. Richard Chase was the college president at that time. He was very amiable toward students in general, and he seemed to be in favor of the ex-offender scholarship program. He approached me one day, in his typical fashion, and asked, "Well, how did you like High Road?"

Because I felt so at ease, I said, "To be honest, I hated it!"

He smiled, pondering for a moment, and responded, "Well, let me ask you, would you do it again?"

"Dr. Chase," I said, "with all due respect, let me say something to you. If you come with me, and we do it together, I would do it again."

He just cracked up with laughter, "No, I won't go." He knew where I was coming from! He talked to me personally and helped me feel at home in Wheaton, and I was thankful for that.

CULTURAL ADJUSTMENT

Home was now a dorm room in Saint Hall, my first real student dormitory experience, because I actually slept in that room! It was located on the first floor, way at the end of the hall. It was the last room, right by the exit door. I supposed the room was conveniently located in the event I was expelled. In a way I found it funny, and yet I didn't. I was learning what it meant to be different, and sometimes treated differently because I was so different.

This was my first experience living among mostly Western-European, light-skinned, English-speaking people. I had spent my whole life among Cubans who always spoke Spanish. My animated expressions of enthusiasm and emotion were a novelty to people at first, but that soon wore off, and I realized that I would have to put forth a lot more effort to be understood by these folks. I had to speak, think, and write in English now, and my brain was programmed in Spanish, still having to translate everything. My brain was on overload. Between my accent and my stuttering, it was a miracle that I communicated with anyone correctly during those first few months.

Old Testament Criticism was a required class for Bible majors, taught by Dr. Andy Hill. Early in the semester, a discussion caused me to mention that I had been to jail. With my heavy Spanish accent, the word came out *yail*. Before he had time to recognize the double meaning, Dr. Hill blurted out, "Manny, I didn't know that you had been to Yale!" I don't think he knew I had been to "yail," either. That became a standard one-liner with me, and a good icebreaker for meeting new people.

I made acquaintances pretty easily and left a lasting impression, but not always a positive one. Physical education was a graduation requirement: one credit hour that included swimming. When test day came, Dr. Bud Williams, my instructor, reminded all of us, "The test is fifty yards each way, and it shouldn't take long for you experienced swimmers," which I thought I was. Each of us swam alone with the rest of the class observing.

My turn came, so I was at the edge in my swimming trunks, and I put my goggles on, although I don't know why I thought I needed goggles. Coach Williams said, "Step up . . . take your mark . . . GO!" When I jumped into the pool, my goggles went up, my trunks went down, and everyone watching got a surprise. I had to ask for another chance, but first I had to swim all the way down to the bottom of the pool to get my trunks. I guess I didn't tie them well enough, and, oh yeah, it was a coed class, so young women were watching the whole fiasco. I knew better than to jump in like that with goggles on, but poor judgment prevailed.

SOME SPIRITUAL MENTORS

In matters of spiritual discipline, my judgment was better. I took advantage of any opportunity I had to pray or focus on God's Word. Dr. Jim Rogers was my professor for statistics and later for educational psychology. He held a devotional on Friday mornings for statistics class, and though the class was large, we connected well during the devotional time.

Dr. Rogers was a very private man, but he took a special liking to me. He invited me to his home, and he took me to White Sox games. He showed a genuine interest in how God was going to use me, and he knew what I was going through with my kids, that I was not able to see them. He and his wife, Evelyn, became good friends to me, and later to my wife, Barbara, as well.

One day a week, Chaplain Hutz and I would fast during the lunch hour and pray for revival on Wheaton's campus. Before long there were many students joining us and even a few faculty members. We put a prayer basket in the foyer at the back of the chapel so people who wanted to write a prayer request could drop it in the basket. I collected the requests, and a team of people— some staff, some faculty, some fellow students— spent time every day praying for those requests. Hutz says I was really the "instigator" of the project, but he wanted to come alongside to support and encourage me. As it turned out, it was very encouraging for him as well.

At Trinity Baptist Church, Hutz was the associate pastor under the senior pastor, John Armstrong. Hutz invited me to attend not long after I became a student, and I enjoyed the fellowship there. Hutz had a strong influence in my life as my pastor, my chaplain, and my friend. He shaped me in lots of ways, because he understood the academic environment and the theological environment in which I was growing, and he helped me apply it all in the real world. He taught me to guard my heart from distractions that could douse the fiery passion God had given me.

My plan for summer school in 1989 focused on classes held in Jerusalem. I had approval from the scholarship program to take fourteen credit hours, if I could get a travel permit from the Bureau of Prisons. My parole officer (PO) used to come to campus to see me, which was a great blessing, since I didn't have any practical way to get to Downers Grove where the federal office was. We sat in my room at Saint Hall and had long talks, sometimes for two or three hours. He told me that summer school in Israel was out of the question. I would never get approved to leave the country on parole. He was not even willing to process a request. I didn't argue with him. I just said I would pray about it.

Dr. Hassel Bullock was in charge of the Wheaton in the Holy Lands course, though he was not teaching the class that summer. Dr. Arthur Rupprechect and Dr. Julius Scott were, and they all supported my desire to go. Dr. Bullock wrote a letter to my PO imploring him to grant me permission. Dr. Bullock personally guaranteed that everything would be OK. That letter was so convincing that my PO filed the papers and defended me to his superiors. The decision was not his to make, but he gave it his best effort, and they issued the permit. What a miraculous answer to prayer.

Before I could leave the country, I had to have a physical examination and inoculations. I went to see Dr. Richard Pinney at the health clinic on campus. Somewhere in the conversation with him I mentioned my ex-wife, Cecilia, and I told him the whole story, including the part about her husband and their new child. The point was that I hadn't seen my children in almost three years. I told Dr. Pinney, "I am praying and expecting God to give me back my ex-wife."

He jumped all over me. He said, "Stop punishing yourself. God is not going to do that! Grow up," he exhorted. "God is not going to destroy another family to give back anything to you. God will open up other doors for you." And that set me free. The Holy Spirit used Dr. Pinney that day to release me. I was hanging onto what I thought God should do, instead of trusting God to do what was best. I confessed and repented and let Cecilia go. As much as I tried to prepare myself for whatever God might do, I never imagined what was next.

Dr. Rupprechect and Dr. Scott became my surrogate parole officers in Israel. We also traveled to Cairo, Egypt, and Athens, Greece, but I didn't need supervision anymore then, because my parole expired on July 13, 1989—the same day I met Barbara Linde.

9

Barbara
LINDE MILL

BARBARA WAS SENT TO ME by God Himself. Early in our marriage I began to affectionately call her my human-holy-spirit, because she speaks truth to me, and she challenges me, even in thinking more biblically. She is not only my wife, but she is my friend, and I love her more than I love life itself.

One thing about Barbara is that she doesn't compromise. She does not side with her husband just because he is her husband. We have learned many things from each other. One thing I know is that if I cannot love my wife as Christ loved the church, then I cannot be a servant leader. My own house has to be in order, so Barbara is a reflection of how Manny Mill really is. How I treat her validates my character, and how she cares for me validates hers. Barbara is more committed to the calling God gave us than I am. We are committed to put God first in our lives. We married with the Holy Spirit's assurance that we could serve the Lord better together than separately.

I don't want to tell how I met Barbara. She needs to tell this part of the story in her own words, so please listen to Barbara Linde Mill speak about herself and how she met her husband, Manny. . . .

BARBARA'S STORY

In the spring of 1989, I sensed that the Lord was bringing a change in my life, and at the urging of my boss at Philadelphia Biblical University (PBU), Don McCullough, I took a short-term biblical geography course at the American Institute of Holy Lands Studies, now called Jerusalem University College. I had been to Israel once before, but I was really looking forward to this trip, thinking it might lead to a master's degree and a teaching career in biblical geography, a subject that stirred my passion, as did the study of God's Word.

Additionally, I was offered two different church ministry opportunities, and I hoped to discern direction from the Holy Spirit very soon. In fact, I was so certain that something was going to happen on this trip that I contemplated the possibility of my own death. Terrorist activities in the Middle East made that thought more than an idle concern, so I wrote out funeral arrangements and left them tucked away in a box where I knew my parents would find them. In a sense I did die, because life as that former Barbara Linde came to an end. A whole new chapter began.

HOW WE MET

Manny was at the Institute taking a course called Wheaton in the Holy Lands. Already several weeks into their studies, most of the class went on to Rome. Manny stayed behind for an archaeological dig, because he could get two additional college credits, since his goal was to get as many credits as he could, as fast as possible. He had been out digging that day, and had to be out there again early the next morning, so he was already in bed when our bus arrived in Mount Zion, Jerusalem, about 10:30 on a Thursday evening.

Our group was told to expect a shuttle to transport our luggage from the bus drop-off to the gate of the Institute. We arrived on the only day during the entire summer that the shuttle happened to be broken. The Institute staff asked the young men in Manny's dorm to help us. Manny did not comply. He selfishly stayed in bed, ignoring the request, but he told me later, "The Holy Spirit convicted me, and I had to get up." At last he emerged and asked, "Who needs help?"

As leader of the group, I made sure that everybody else had been taken care of first. To my dismay, I was standing alone. Although I thought I didn't need his help or want it, the only polite thing to do was accept. "Me," I said in a tentative voice. He carried my suitcases and immediately began talking, which surprised me. In that short walk from the bus to the door of my room, I heard a synopsis of his life story and the invitation, "I'd like to tell you more sometime." I made no comment about when that sometime might be, but he definitely piqued my interest.

The next evening, the institute held a Friday-night vespers service, kind of like an *Erev Shabbot* service. As groups came and went, so did service leaders. Word went out that there was no pianist for vespers. Somehow I got roped into playing, and I am not a piano player. In fact, a very qualified couple was there, a pastor and wife who team-played keyboards in their home church. Why they held back I don't know, but after I tried my best, they quickly volunteered for the rest of the services.

I was nervous enough about trying to play the piano. Then through my peripheral vision, I was aware of that guy I had just met the night before, trying to maneuver a seat close to me. I was woman enough to figure that one out. He placed the chair nearer to the piano bench than the first row afforded him. When he sat down, the chair broke, and the next thing I knew, he was on the floor with all sorts of commotion. I noticed that he had a bent toward being the center of attention, regardless of his objective.

Saturday night, after *Shabbot* was over, the ice cream shops and all the stores in the Jewish section opened back up. My friend from PBU and I debated whether it was safe for the two of us to go by ourselves. Through our open window we overheard the Wheaton group standing in the courtyard below discussing plans to go to Ben Yehuda Street, so I called out the window and asked if we could join them. From that scenario, Manny says that I asked him out first.

We joined their group and walked along the street together. Walking back, Manny stuck to me like glue, and I tried to get rid of him. Finally, he just asked, "Why are you avoiding me?" He was refreshingly honest, but I also thought, *Oh, don't be so blunt!* and I tried to brush it off.

"I'm not ignoring you," I quipped, and he rebutted, "Yes, you are." Inadvertently, instead of maintaining a cautious distance, I hooked him further.

He was very interested in getting to know

me better and explained his strategy, knowing how many days he had left at the Institute and what our schedules were like. "I am willing to do whatever it takes. Can we meet for breakfast and talk before I go off to the dig and you go off to class?"

I agreed to meet, and then he asked if we could go together to the Sunday evening worship service. I said I would go *if* I could find somebody to swap dish washing, because Sunday was my turn.

Everyone at the Institute took turns for a night of dish washing. Unknown to me, Manny inquired of everybody on campus. He had backups for his backups for his backups. If I came back empty-handed, he was prepared. The entire campus waited to hear my answer so they could know whether they were free to make plans for the night. When I announced that I had found someone on my own willing to swap the night with me, everyone was relieved of their obligation to Manny.

So our first official "date" was the Sunday evening church service at the YMCA that sits just across the Hinnom Valley from the Institute. The distance was not terribly far, but it was quite a hike because the path went down and then steeply up, up, up. Manny's pace up the other side of the mountain caused me to recognize early on, *I can't keep up with this man!*

The church service that night was incredible. Manny was obviously and genuinely interested in worshiping his Lord Jesus. Such passion for God was extremely refreshing and very attractive to me. I decided that maybe this interesting man who seemed rather pushy was worth getting to know better.

Everybody attending the Institute became like a small family, so we all wound up sitting together at meal times. Manny and I sat near each other at breakfast and then again at dinner, and we talked, and talked, and talked. One of the older women from PBU pulled me aside one afternoon and expressed concern that this guy was moving in on me too fast. But then she spent the rest of our conversation telling me how she pictured the two of us in ministry together and how exciting that was for her! We laughed a lot over the whole situation, but I appreciated her insight.

COURTSHIP AND QUESTIONS

Manny did not hide his intentions; he was looking for a courtship. We didn't spend time with cordialities, like favorite foods and favorite movies. I was out to grill him theologically, so we spent a lot of time discussing Scripture and doctrine and his goals for future ministry. I also wanted to know about his past.

In my theological background, divorce was a serious issue and remarriage was not an option, regardless of the circumstances of the divorce. One of my close girlfriends had faced these issues with a divorced man, which caused me to wrestle along with her, in an abstract sort of way. I never expected to confront it myself, and the challenge to work it through was tough, not just for me, but for my parents and colleagues at the college. If Cecilia had not already remarried, I would have walked away immediately. I knew where my heart was leading me. My head needed to make some choices before my heart got too carried away. Our meetings were not all rosy. Manny was not one for frivolous romance, so my practicality was a good match in that respect.

My mom knew immediately that I was "in trouble" when I called to tell her I had met someone. In my spirit of self-reliance, I rarely called home while traveling, let alone long-distance from Israel. I wanted to give them a heads-up and ask if Manny could stay at our house for a few days and meet them.

So what's one of the first things my parents did when their grown daughter asked to bring a man home to meet them? They shared the situation with their pastor, and he told them, "Oh, I know somebody who probably knows Manny. I'll call to get the lowdown on this guy."

Pastor Bill Schmidt served on the board of

SIM, an international mission, along with Dr. James Kraakevik, who was the director of the Billy Graham Center at Wheaton College. The ex-offender scholarship was one of the programs under his domain. Of course, he knew Manny. After Manny's nine months on campus, who didn't know Manny! Lots of checking was going on behind the scenes for both of us, even before we got back from Israel. What impressed me most was that it didn't bother Manny. In fact, he welcomed inspection, except for the tedious kind he had to do in his archaeology class.

Manny's digging assignment was in some Roman tombs. "I found some great stuff!" he told me one day "—a pair of gold earrings and a ring from the Roman period." I knew he didn't really like the work, which amused me for some reason.

"Sifting. Sifting," he went on. "You have to do a lot of sifting. No good for me. Requires a lot of patience. Too boring, but it gave me a glimpse of true archaeology."

Most people never experience an archaeological dig and would never want to, so I gave him credit for trying to appreciate the uniqueness of the opportunity. I couldn't resist teasing him just a little. "Isn't everything on that dig from the Roman period?" I asked, showing more interest than he could muster.

"Not at all," he said with a smile. "I found you, and you're from the modern period."

Manny's last day in Israel was not particularly emotional for us. We got up really early and stood overlooking the Western Wall in order to watch the sun rise over Jerusalem. His bus was leaving right after that. He planned to meet me in New York when I flew home, so we were not facing a lengthy separation. Yet I was sad to see him go since he was such a significant part of this whole Israel experience. He waved madly out the window of the shuttle bus while I mechanically waved back, dazed from the whirlwind I'd just experienced. I needed time to breathe and think things over, so the next week-and-a-half I buckled down to finish my schoolwork, and that was good medicine.

MANNY AND MY PARENTS MEET

Before I knew it, my parents were at Kennedy International Airport, ready to drive the PBU group back home. They were waiting right in the terminal, and Manny was there too, but he had not been introduced yet. Up in the air, our plane was filled with anticipation, knowing my parents were coming to pick us up. Teasing went on about the drama unfolding before our eyes. "We're going to see the moment when Manny and Barbara meet up and Barbara's parents meet Manny." The excitement mounted. We went so far as to plan how we all would walk off the plane and in what order. I had to be last so everyone else could be there to watch the show. They knew who to look for, but Manny and my parents didn't. The atmosphere approached frenzied by the time we landed.

Meanwhile, my parents surveyed the crowd waiting at the gate, wondering which one of these guys was *the* guy. They didn't know whether he was tall, dark, and handsome, or short, fat, and bald, and he was neither. Not exceptionally tall, not fat at all, but pleasingly bald, he stood not far from them. Later, Dad recalled, "Yup, the first time I met Manny was on our thirty-ninth wedding anniversary. Quite a present!" To no one's surprise, Manny talked most of the way home, as my dad drove and the rest of us listened in on the conversation. After everyone had been dropped off, we drove home. Manny sat down on the living room sofa and told my parents he wanted to marry me. We had known each other barely a week; they had known each other a couple of hours. Manny said, "Ask me anything you want."

They could tell he genuinely meant that, and I was pleased with the way my parents handled him. My mother did ask him questions, including some hard questions, and he was very open and honest. That's been him, since day one. *Coram Deo* is the phrase that he lives by, *openly before the face of God*. Sometimes this in-your-face person was hard to accept, especially since I was raised in a culture where pretense was part of etiquette. More often, I found his unpretentious disposition appealing, and his laughter was irresistible. At the end of the day, my parents reflected, "Thirty-nine years ago we never dreamed we would have a day like this!"

My mother remembered how often she prayed for my future husband. Mom confessed to our pastor, "She was past thirty, and I knew she wanted to be married. I prayed that somewhere out there the Lord had a nice, Christian young man that loved the Lord like Barbara did. You know, to be her husband. Then, she met Manny, and bit by bit I found out he was an ex-con, had been married and divorced, had children, and he was a Cuban!"

Unable to repress his wry smile, Pastor Schmidt suggested, "That should teach you to be more specific in your prayers."

"Nah," Mom chuckled. "The important part is there. He loves the Lord. And he makes her happy."

THE DECISION

I suspected that Manny was "the one," but the defining moment for me came while watching a videotape. Manny did a taped interview with Dr. Joel Nederhood for a program called

Faith 20. He was very excited about it and sent me a copy right away. I played the tape during lunch with a friend of mine, in our little conference room at the college. We were listening to him elaborate on his testimony. She turned to me and exclaimed with enthusiasm, "To think this is the man that wants to marry you!" Suddenly, the reality of the moment hit me. "I've got a choice to make."

I tried to imagine what my life would be like, having known Manny Mill, if now I shut him out. How could I go on living, knowing that this vibrant person was somewhere out there, apart from me?

Not long after, the confirmation I sought came. My devotional reading was in 1 Chronicles. When I got to chapter 28, King David speaking to Solomon said, "Be strong and courageous." These words really struck me. I was concerned about what other people might think of me, a girl from Philadelphia Biblical University marrying a Cuban, divorced, ex-convict. I was not being strong and courageous. I was being weak. I continued reading, "Do not be afraid or discouraged, for the Lord God, my God, is with you. He will not fail you or forsake you" (v. 20). I didn't notice how much these words resembled the verse that God gave Manny at his conversion (Hebrews 13:5). How foundational this truth became to both our lives!

LIFE CHANGE AND ADJUSTMENTS

Deep down inside, I was a homebody. As much as I pretended to be dramatic and daring, I didn't like change, so having to adapt in adventurous situations was forced rather than embraced. Coming home was the part of traveling I liked best. The one thing Manny Mill guaranteed to promote was change.

We were already on our honeymoon when the stress of imminent change became almost unbearable. I had made my commitment and I was pleased about that, but now I had to face the fact that I was days away from leaving the only home I had ever had and all the people I ever knew. God was preparing me, showing me "I can take care of you." I left my physical family, but when we came to Wheaton, God provided a spiritual family through my employment at World Relief. Often I felt I should have paid them for allowing me to work there. They were such a blessing. God was showing me "I can provide." We needed that confidence in years to come.

Cultural change was probably my biggest adjustment. Cubans are loud. Manny was no exception, exceedingly joyful and boisterous. I came from a basically quiet household. We could be loud in our own way, but by comparison, we were reserved. My father observed,

"When Manny sat here and called his mom in Union City, I thought he was trying to shout all the way to New Jersey without using the telephone."

Manny's effervescence was attractive, but living with it in daily doses was an adjustment that broadened me. My comfortable little world where I was all closed in no longer existed. My way was certainly not the only way. Traveling to Israel opened my eyes to other cultures and enabled me to recognize that God's blessings extended to many more people groups than my little clan of Pennsylvanian Christians in the suburbs of Philadelphia.

One of Manny's professors told me a story about their trip to southern Greece, and it really drove this point home for me. The class was staying at a charming hotel near the town of Patras, located on the beach at the mouth of the Gulf of Corinth. Manny woke early to pray down on the beach. The sandy shore was completely deserted except for a very dignified Nigerian student at the west end, sitting quietly with his Bible and obviously praying. At the other end of the beach, on a little boat dock, was Manny. Manny assumed that this secluded beach was a safe place to be loud. He walked back and forth, raising his arms and gesturing wildly as he talked with God, apparently having a joyfully noisy time of prayer. Dr. Scott and his wife happened to step out on the balcony of the hotel. They observed the demeanor of the two students as a wonderful example of the rich diversity within the church. The contrasting imagery was so striking that Dr. Scott couldn't get it out of his mind. Both accepted the other, demonstrating unity of the body of Christ. The godly Nigerian in stillness and silence, and the godly Cuban, animated and thunderous, praying with equal sincerity—and Jesus approved both. I recognized that I related to the Nigerian student's style of prayer more than my own husband's style.

I also experienced a small taste of what it was like to be a minority, as an Anglo woman amidst all Cubans at times, and later in our ministry, as a white woman among all men of color. I had a lot of growing up and changing to do, and Manny was very patient and loving, especially when I didn't improve very rapidly.

Recently, Manny phoned to tell me that Chuck Colson sent an email, responding to Jude's interview questions for this book. I knew he would be bubbling over with enthusiasm when he came home, but I had had a pretty rough day. I was just beginning to think about dinner, and I was not quite prepared to greet him yet. So when I saw his car pulling into the driveway, I ran to our bedroom to pause, to literally take a couple of deep breaths so I could be ready to meet my husband at the door. As I was running away, I caught myself thinking how strange it was to run away from my husband. Still, I retreated as far away as I could get, but I wasn't quick enough.

Manny came barreling through the door like a little boy anxious to show all that he had done at school that day. When he didn't find me waiting at the door, he charged into the bedroom waving the printed message in the air. He handed me the paper, and my eyes immediately fell to the end of the page where I read, "One of the things that needs to be written about Manny is the story of Barbara, his wife. How anybody could harness this bundle of energy called Manny Mill is beyond me. She is a saint."

I broke into hysterical laughter, tears and all, thinking to myself, *She handles him by running away!* What great timing. I laughed so hard and so long that Manny got on the phone to Jude, totally perplexed, wanting to know what he should do about his hysterical wife.

I am no "saint," in the sense that Chuck meant, the picture of piety and virtue. I know the depravity of my own soul apart from Jesus Christ. I am a redeemed sinner, grateful for the outpouring of God's amazing grace.

When the dust settles at the end of the day, there is a joy deep down in my heart. The desire of Barbara Linde to find her ultimate place of ministry was fulfilled as God revealed His plans for a ministry of reconciliation together. I am truly blessed to be Mrs. Manny Mill.

10

◆

Courtship and
MARRIAGE

I CONSULTED WITH MANY people about Barbara, because I learned quickly in my young Christian life that God works through people, especially to affirm direction from the Holy Spirit. I was looking for discernment, not approval. Interestingly enough, some people felt they wanted to "check her out" for me, which spoke highly of their ability to put my past under the blood of Christ. I had not thought about my best interests being just as important as hers. Wow!

Of course, when it came time for me to marry, I wanted Ken Wessner's blessing. He and Norma accepted Barbara with the same warmth that they showed to me.

BARBARA MEETS CHAPLAIN CORDERO

An important affirmation came from my former prison chaplain in Allenwood. Barbara and I planned to attend a Prison Fellowship Banquet at a hotel in Baltimore, Maryland, so I could introduce Barbara to Chuck Colson. The hotel was two or three hours by car from Barbara's home in Philadelphia, depending on traffic. We drove down early in comfortable travel clothes and enjoyed a walk around Baltimore before dressing for dinner. I left Barbara in the hotel lobby while I took our traveling clothes back to the car. As people arrived, Barbara observed, in her unassuming way, the name tags of several guests including Gordon Barnes and Manny Cordero. Though I had spoken of them often, Barbara had never met them, and there they were greeting each other. She barely contained herself and anxiously watched for my return. We had no idea they would be there. What a wonderful opportunity this became to introduce the woman I hoped to marry. When I introduced them, Manny Cordero piped up and said to Barbara, "You and I have got to talk."

Before the banquet started, Barbara went for a long walk, listening to Chaplain Cordero's version of the standard message, "I've got to caution you about marrying this man." She'd heard that one before! But the two of them taking time to get to know each other meant a lot to me. Chaplain was very open with Barbara. I wanted them to have that freedom. He told her everything about me, and offered her valuable insight. "Make sure that he keeps himself grounded in a biblically sound church and surrounded by a group of strong, godly men."

"Well, the local church has always been important to me, and if Manny didn't believe in that, I wouldn't be with him," Barbara reassured him. Chaplain brought up the cultural changes ahead, wondering if she had given that any thought. He being a Puerto Rican and I being Cuban testified to the power of the Gospel to produce cross-cultural unity. He joked with her, but he was serious when it came to recognizing what the Lord was doing in my life. "He is a man of God," Chaplain told her, "and God has His hand on your Manny Mill."

Barbara and Chaplain Cordero wrapped up their chat, and we all took seats for a joyful banquet together. Afterward, Chuck Colson was very pleased to meet my future wife. She thought ahead to bring her copy of his book *Born Again,* and he graciously wrote a personal inscription to Barbara.

OTHERS FROM MY PAST MEET BARBARA

Hand in hand Barbara and I walked along the waterfront, reflecting on the events of the day, when a carousel came into view. I confessed that I had never ridden one. The hour was late, but Barbara insisted, "The lights are still on! We have to do it."

All the parts of the carousel were very ornately painted. Unnaturally colored animals with eerie expressions on some of their faces galloped up and down burnished poles. All the gold leaf sparked a memory of Cuban statues. Barbara enjoyed sharing my first carousel ride, until she noticed a man looking our way, with the kind of look that says you think you know someone, but you're not sure if you should say anything. He approached us. He was one of the brothers from Allenwood, and when I asked him about his relationship with Christ, he seemed uncomfortable and kind of sidestepped the question. In prison, he was really involved in church, but obviously he wasn't hooked up out here. I think he was genuinely glad to see me and meet Barbara, but not glad to be confronted with his weak spiritual condition. As we headed back to our car, we discussed what we might do to encourage him further.

We were just crossing a deserted street when a car turned down the block. The driver slowed, and as he rolled down his window, Barbara whispered, "Oh, my goodness, is this safe?"

We heard him call out, "Manny? Manny Mill? Is that you? It's me, Bob Brantley!"

"Barbara, this is another guy who did time with me in prison!" He had been on the Washington Discipleship team as my chaperone. We stood in the street and talked for quite a while. We intended to be home at a reasonable hour, but pulled into the Lindes' driveway early the next morning. No one was waiting up to interrogate me or anything like that.

CHRISTIAN FELLOWSHIP OF CRYSTAL LAKE

Christian Fellowship of Crystal Lake also acted on my behalf. We were already engaged by the time I brought Barbara out to visit Pastor Cozad, Mama Libby, and the rest of my Christian family there. We may have seemed wild and crazy, having just met in July and planning a January wedding. Yet God provided peaceful confirmations all along the way. A few of the women grilled Barbara about her faith and doctrine. They wanted to be sure that she was a strong believer. I was quite charismatic then, and Barbara was quite conservative, so how would we blend? Because we based our courtship on our love for Christ and our kindred theology, we had the rest of our lives to learn the fine points together.

Despite her different background and different gift mix, Christian Fellowship of Crystal Lake warmly embraced Barbara. A few uncomfortable moments did not hinder Barbara's appreciation for the fact that no one assumed anything and spoke frankly about what was on their hearts. Her conservative upbringing was a positive influence in many ways, but particularly when she moved into the Wheaton community. She adjusted easily, and ultimately she helped me to better understand many aspects of the still unfamiliar culture.

ENGAGED

Maybe I need to explain how we finally got engaged. Barbara knew I was flying out to see her on September 22, and she probably suspected that the official proposal was coming, but neither of us expected the curveball that Hurricane Hugo threw. Or should I say blew? Barbara's parents had planned to go out for the evening, so Barbara hoped to have a nice, romantic dinner for two at the house. Then Hurricane Hugo hit. Most flights departing from the west were delayed, but we didn't hit bad weather until we approached Pennsylvania. All the planes diverted from South Carolina converged in Philadelphia's airspace and caused an awful traffic jam.

My plane circled over Philadelphia for more

than two hours before we could land. By that time, I wondered if Barbara would still be there when I deplaned. My patience was all but gone, and I didn't have much to begin with, so when I saw my beautiful Barbara standing there, faithfully waiting for me, my heart about burst with joy.

"My parents canceled their plans because of the storm," Barbara said with a laugh, "so who wants to have a romantic dinner with my folks right there!" That was all the encouragement I needed to pull her off to the side.

Under an escalator, I dropped to one knee and managed to open the ring box right in her face before I blurted out, "Will you marry me?" And guess what? She said yes.

PLANNING FOR THE WEDDING

The next morning we sat down with Mr. and Mrs. Linde to get their blessing on our wedding plans, and suggested January 6, 1990, as the date. Wheaton College would be between semesters and, miraculously, a married student housing apartment was coming available in mid-year. Our commitment was for real. We were not eighteen-year-old kids. So, why wait?

Mrs. Linde wanted to delay, protesting, "Why so soon?" Our courtship was still relatively recent news, and she had not yet adjusted to the fact that she was going to have to give up her daughter.

Mrs. Linde turned to Mr. Linde and said, "Well, aren't you going to say something? I think it's too soon!"

After he thought for a moment, Mr. Linde answered, "I can understand their reasoning. If they want to get married on the sixth, I think that's fine."

After agreeing to the January 6 date, Mrs. Linde ordered us to talk to her mother, anxious to hear what her response would be. We went right away to find out. What a surprise when Grandmom in all seriousness asked, "Why are you waiting so long?"

Three months to plan a wedding was a little tight, but no one thought that was impossible, not with Barbara Linde, executive office administrator *extraordinaire* at the helm. Her dress was a *Jacque Penné Original* (aka J.C. Penney) which was in an affordable price range. Of course, anything she chose would have looked fabulous to me. The Lindes' church sanctuary was already decorated with trees, garland, and wreaths from the holidays, so our flower expense was minimal. PBU was between semesters, leaving the auditorium available for a reception. The kitchen staff kindly agreed to work on their day off to cater the reception. I think that was a reflection of how highly Barbara was thought of on campus. The January 6 date was especially significant to me because it was also *Three Kings Day,* a Cuban holiday celebrated much like Christmas in the U.S.

At one of Barbara's final fittings, her bridal gown was properly pressed for the first time and she realized just how puffy the sleeves really were. Barbara turned to her mom and said, "I can't put a coat on over this dress. How am I going to do that?"

Her mother laughed, using humor to get her digs in, like only a mother can. "Well, you're the one that picked the January wedding date. You'll just have to figure it out!"

I assured Mrs. Linde that I would ask the Lord for beautiful weather. God blessed us big time for a January day in Bristol, Pennsylvania; the temperature was miraculously in the fifties. The woman who cut Barbara's hair also loaned her a long white cape, but Barbara never wore it. No one needed a coat.

THE WEDDING DAY

Our invitations said the wedding started at noon, and Barbara was ready at noon! Sunlight streamed through the glass windows of the church as if it were a sign of God's approval. Around two hundred people attended, but I didn't know many of them. Almost everyone knew Barbara, even those on the groom's side. My family came from New Jersey, and some of my PFM discipleship friends came too. I don't think Barbara ever imagined her wedding day populated with ex-convict guests, but I could already see the special way she loved these brothers in Christ.

No one needed to remind me that I did not deserve Barbara. She was above and beyond anything I could think up or ask for, and God gave her to me. She sang at our wedding. Everyone was blessed by the music, but I felt like she sang just to me. We were intentional about planning for our ceremony. Wedding music was no exception, chosen carefully, with special attention to the words. Barbara chose lyrics that were so personal, and so fitting for the day. We had no idea what God was going to do in our lives, yet the lyrics of openness to God's leading in times of crisis and availability to offer God's hospitality and love continued to fit as God revealed our future ministry!

Yes, we loved each other, but throughout the ceremony we tried to communicate that we as a couple would be a better vessel for God's service than if we continued serving separately. Two pastors conducted the service. One presented a clear gospel message from our favorite text, 2 Corinthians 5, also engraved in our wedding rings and in my college ring, given to me by Barbara. The other pastor did our vows.

My big responsibilities that day were to make sure the best man had the rings and to say the vows. What an embarrassment, in front of all those people, speaking to my wife, and I couldn't say the words because my stuttering was so bad. My mouth tried to shape the words, but I shook hard and nothing came out. The pastor had to stop the whole wedding and break it down to my level. Barbara said he even reached out and touched my arm to reassure me that we would get through it. "Manny, it's OK," he said, "—just say the words." He began again, three or four times it seemed. I felt like saying the vows took longer than the whole rest of the ceremony. I just couldn't speak, not even little simple words. "Repeat after me," Pastor said again, but I couldn't. It was unbelievable.

Mrs. Linde was probably not alone as she prayed silently in her seat. "They were the longest wedding vows I ever sat through," she told us later. "I thought they would never end, just because Manny had such a terrible time. I wished Pastor would have cut it short. You would have still been married, you know."

Well, maybe I was nervous, but normally I didn't get too nervous in public. God was telling me, "Just trust Me. I will do it for you." After a while, I think Barbara wanted to laugh. She was struggling with me. She was kind of prodding me, "Come on, Manny. Say it! I know you love me. Say it! I know you want to marry me. Say it!" But I couldn't say it. That day, I knew I was a really weak, feeble person who had nothing to offer. I felt like a nobody and not very confident. I bet a lot of people identified with that. I was a willing person, though, and God could use any willing person. Ultimately God helped me and I got through the vows, one word at a time.

Barbara and I didn't get any of our cake. By the time we thought about eating a piece, none was left. Then we went back to the Lindes' house. I didn't know if opening gifts after the reception was an American tradition or not, but they told me to do it, so I did it.

Planning the honeymoon was my responsibility, but Barbara didn't mind helping me. From the start of our relationship it seemed that we didn't do much "by the book" anyway. We knew another couple who had just been away at a bed and breakfast place. Barbara thought it was worth a try to call for a reservation. "It's Christmastime. Who goes away to a bed and breakfast at this time of year?"

The weekend following New Year's Day was the only vacancy available in January. Chestnut Hill was the name of the place, in Milford, New Jersey. It was beautiful, perfect for our four-day getaway.

When we moved back to Wheaton as Mr. and Mrs. Manny Mill, Barbara unpacked some things that I had been given a year before to help get me started on my own. In a box with dishes, someone included magazines on entertaining. Barbara opened one magazine and showed me a picture. "This living room looks familiar." It was the living room of the main house at the bed and breakfast. Barbara looked at me and said, "Would you ever have dreamt that a year later you would be at this place on your honeymoon?"

11

·

Postprison
MINISTRY

I N EXODUS 4:10 WE LEARN that Moses
had a speech impediment. No one knows exactly what that was, but Moses said, "I am slow
of speech and tongue." That was an accurate description of my own speech impediment. Although stuttering was not the excuse I used, my
first response to God's specific instruction was
also like Moses': "Send someone else to do it." I
had other plans.

Because of his close involvement with
Prison Fellowship Ministries, Ken Wessner
hoped that I might minister to Spanish-speaking inmates. His heart's desire was to see that
their special needs were met, and he thought
I might become a director within PFM to
make that happen.

My heart's desire was to be a federal prison chaplain, like my dear friend and mentor, Manny Cordero. I felt I could impact Spanish-speaking brothers better in that venue. Only two federal chaplains at that time had Latino ethnicity, and the prison population had a growing Latino segment. Yes, I wanted to do something good and noble with my life, and Ken wanted me to do something good and noble, but God had something better planned for me. I was still looking to myself for security and purpose. God wanted me to depend on Him. He had so much more to teach me. I finally acquiesced.

THE BIRTH OF KOINONIA HOUSE

Barbara and I responded to God's sovereign call in 1990, and by His grace we began to cultivate this unique postprison ministry, Koinonia House of DuPage County, Inc. Koinonia House (which means "belonging together in mutual partnership") is a family-home-based ministry of biblical discipleship for Christians coming out of prison. Postprison ministry is the term we chose to distinguish our ministry from more institutional types of services, like aftercare and halfway house.

God gave us the command to provide a ministry that *waited at the gate* when a Christian man or woman was released from prison. The idea was to *bring people to live with a family* where they could be fed and clothed and *taught the Word of God.* We connected them to a local church fellowship, which provided additional support in many ways, including two mentors to assist in their development as Christians. An important concept to remember was that no matter how long a person had been a Christian inside prison, he or she did not know how to live as a Christian outside prison, in the world. Another essential concept was that this transformation took place in the context of relationships. By recreating a family atmosphere, these men and women experienced healthy family-like relationships that helped heal old wounds and prepared them to be the Christian parents that their own children needed. Their mentors and their local church body became a Christian extended family where receiving and giving appropriate nurture and support would become a new way of life.

What I soon realized was that Koinonia House, in a nutshell, was a graphic example of what Jesus meant when He commanded us in Luke 10:27, "Love your neighbor as yourself." I could have written a whole book about all the things God did in and through our little postprison ministry, so I have tried to limit this chapter to a few of the incidents that contributed to my personal growth and joy in Christ.

BRIDGING THE GAP

The inspiration for Koinonia House truly began when I was released. The more I prayed about ministry, the more God spoke to me to do something about this most neglected segment of the body of Christ, Christians coming out of prison. Hundreds of ministries go *in* to prison and minister. Very few allow themselves to think about what happens at the release gate. Something needed to be done, but not many were willing to try, and of those who tried, many gave up quickly because of discouraging results and lack of support resources.

When I was released, my experience was unusual. God provided Christians to bridge the gap for me. What kind of Christian would I have been without them? Just the fact that my family of origin had become Christians made a huge difference. Many Christian ex-prisoners cannot go home to family members, because they would be drawn back into their old way of life. The need for postprison ministry was compelling, in fact urgent, and God caused us to see it with the eyes of our hearts. When we shared this calling with Ken Wessner, he knew it was from God and he blessed it.

Prison Fellowship offered many types of training seminars for in-prison ministry. Barbara and I flew to Orlando, Florida, and attended marriage seminar training, which was God's providence again. We hoped to visit an aftercare ministry called The Bridge, located in Orlando. We learned firsthand how they minister to Christians after prison. We met several people who became involved in our ministry later on, but at that time, most of them thought I was full of hot air when they heard our plans for ministry. Barbara and I heard the words "you're crazy" more often than we cared to count, especially from our friend, Judge Bob Downing, but we didn't mind. We weren't even that crazy, yet. We did not see the full picture of God's plan for us, personally.

THE BOARD OF DIRECTORS

Back in Wheaton, we gathered a small group to become our Board of Directors and presented our plan for Koinonia House. In the original constitution and bylaws, the board was actually named Board of Control, based on the wisdom of Manny Cordero. I placed myself under the authority of godly Christians who were willing to *control* me, a difficult task and not the usual role of a not-for-profit volunteer board. After Barbara and I calculated a ministry budget, the board said, "Great. Now go raise it." Barbara continued to work at World Relief, and I didn't earn a penny of salary until we raised 70 percent of my approved annual income; and then I received 70 percent of a bimonthly paycheck. My title was Executive Director, and I was the overseer of this new concept in postprison ministry. In a lot of ways, it was like the good old days, Manny Mill the big promoter, networking with people to get the job done; yet now I promoted Jesus instead of myself.

Dr. Hutz Hertzberg was our first board chairman in 1990. We still lived on campus, so we held our first board meeting in our apartment on College Avenue. Hutz was skilled in tact, not the type to get in people's faces. He got in my face, though, when he said, "Manny, I think that you should do this first. I think that you and Barbara should be the ones to live in the house."

"No. No. No!" I answered, emphatically.

Hutz did not quit. "Manny, just pray about it, and think about it."

"No. I refuse to do it." I didn't have to pray about it, or so I thought. I didn't want to do postprison ministry to begin with, let alone live in the house. I ignored Hutz's counsel for a long time. We had another couple chosen to move into the house, as soon as we found a house. I focused on my schoolwork and other aspects of the ministry's development.

PREPARING TO SPEAK FOR GOD

God used many people in my life to build my confidence. Jim Rogers and his wife, Evelyn, found a special way to empower me for future ministry. They sent me to the Hollins Institute in Roanoke, Virginia, for a three-week speech therapy program. I bawled on the phone with Barbara every night, partly because I missed her and our sons so badly, and partly because the work was extremely intense. Difficult as it was, I determined to complete the course. The Rogers had been so gracious, I couldn't disappoint them.

The Holy Spirit encouraged me to be obedient and let Him orchestrate all that I needed. "You do your best. I'll do the rest. I'm going to speak for you." I never thought it would be possible, but God helped me to speak clearly, in English and in Spanish. Ever since I went to therapy, I stopped stuttering while preaching. Therapy did not help my accent, however, so whether or not the pronunciation was clear—that's a different story! If I am very tired, I might struggle a little bit during conversation, but that has been the extent of it.

In the fall of 2002, Barbara and I were on our way to Asheville, North Carolina. The Billy Graham Evangelistic Association invited us to The Cove for a leadership training conference.

The Hollins Institute was a five-minute detour off the main route, so we had to stop. I wanted to show Barbara where I had been. Some staff people were still working there and remembered me. The director came out to greet us personally. I was thrilled to tell them about all that God had done since then, and how much their ministry made a difference in my life.

A HOUSE FOR THE MINISTRY

When we were first putting together the ministry, Ken Wessner arranged a meeting for me with the new president of Prison Fellowship, Tom Pratt, to personally present Koinonia House postprison ministry. I was preparing my presentation and would be flying to Reston, Virginia, the next day when Tom telephoned to ask for help.

Friends of Tom's, a father and son, were scheduled to tour Wheaton College, but their tour guide canceled at the last minute. Tom wanted me to meet them and give the tour. Apparently, the son was considering applying to the college, but Tom wanted more than a typical admissions tour for his friends. I wish my first reaction was, "Of course, Tom, I will be happy to step in!" Instead, I whined to myself about my homework and my preparations for the trip, and I really didn't want to go up campus right then.

Tom told me where to meet them in the Billy Graham Center, which was just a couple of blocks from our apartment, so I agreed to do a quick, forty-five-minute tour. As we were walking together, we bumped into Bud Williams, whom I had met through my High Road adventures. He was familiar with the ministry plans, and he asked me, "How you doin' Manny, with your house?"

"Well, we don't have a house yet," I answered hastily, as I kept the tour moving, "but thank you for asking!"

I didn't think the man or his son heard what transpired. The thought never occurred to me that they had any interest in our ministry plans. They thanked me for the tour, we said our goodbyes, and I hustled off to get back to my own agenda. We didn't exchange phone numbers or anything.

Evidently, the man called Tom that evening at his home, because Tom called me. He was so stunned that he didn't want to wait until he met me the next day. "My friend just called and asked me if you were for real!"

"Wow!" I responded. I didn't know what to think.

Tom relayed, "I told him, yes, he is for real. And he said the Holy Spirit told him he had to do something for you. So I said he should buy you a house."

"And he laughed at you, right?"

"No," Tom continued. "He asked me who else he could talk to that would attest to your character. So, I told him how about Ken Wessner? And I gave him Ken's number. So I guess he will call Ken. I'll see you tomorrow."

In essence, Ken Wessner guaranteed a loan with his word. A week after I met with Tom, the ministry received a check in the mail for $120,000, as a mortgage loan to the ministry. I never saw the man again, but after seven years of mortgage payments, the loan was paid down to $75,000, and he forgave the rest of the debt. His investment also gave the ministry a very favorable credit report.

OTHER EXAMPLES OF GOD'S PROVIDENCE

Tom Pratt and Ken Wessner were examples of the kind of people God sent our way to get the ministry started. We are grateful to God for many people who have had a part, but we are even more grateful for the Holy Spirit who interceded on our behalf. Nothing happened without prayer first, and then God's people who responded, like this man did, to the leading of God's Holy Spirit. I realized that what seemed like an interruption to me was the hand of God moving. God had to show me over and over, and I continued to need His grace as I learned to recognize and submit to His providence on a daily basis.

Not long after we purchased the house, we had some disunity over how the ministry would be run. Conflict was brewing in the community, so the couple who planned to live in the house stepped down and we faced a dilemma. God provided the house and we lost the family. Only then was I willing to consider Hutz's plea to pray about Barbara and me living there first. Not long after that, I knew Hutz was right, but I didn't say anything to Barbara. I just waited until she confirmed to me that the Holy Spirit had spoken. We moved into the house, and the battle with neighbors and the City Council progressed. Barbara and I were the ones God chose to lead this battle, and by His grace, we worked it out, but only after we filed a lawsuit against the city of Wheaton.

Filing suit was a last resort, and I remain convinced that it was necessary. I was truly amazed at all the blessings that came about because of the publicity and the people God sent to defend our case, particularly attorneys like Don Whittaker and Jim Geoly. I cannot count the number of people who have volunteered and supported the Christian residents at Koinonia House over the years, simply because pastors in the Wheaton community came together and supported a cause worth fighting for, religious freedom. Denominational barriers were broken down, racial barriers were broken down, class barriers were broken down, and God did a new thing through this little postprison ministry. Our relationship with the city officials came to be strong and mutually supportive as years passed and the ministry thrived.

Another lesson I had to learn the hard way came at the expense of a stranger. I was on my way to the Wheaton post office, which was a daily errand that I and my two small sons did together. The parking was pretty limited in those days, and often cars waited in line on the street for the next available space. Just as it was my turn to park, a man in another car cut me off and took the parking space. Naturally, I was upset. Quickly, I rolled down my window and called out, "Sir, you just took my parking space!"

He kept walking up the stairs to the post office entrance, while I called out even louder, "Sir, you just took my parking space!" He went right into the post office and never looked back. Finally I got another space. As I walked up the stairs with my boys, the man came out, and I said again, "Sir, you just took my parking space," and he kept on walking. I did not take the hint, and quite loudly called after him, "I am talking to you, sir! You just took my parking space!" The man got into his car and drove away.

As I turned once more toward the post office entrance, another gentleman stopped me. "Excuse me," he said, "Are you Manny Mill?" I nodded. "Shame on you! Aren't you the director of Koinonia House?"

"Yes, yes, I am."

"You should have never spoken to that man that way!"

Oh, man, I didn't know where to hide. I didn't know what to say. I stumbled all over the place, and I had no excuse. Right there I apologized to him and apologized to God, but I could not apologize to the man who drove away. I didn't know who he was. When I got home, I told Barbara what happened and she had no compassion for me. "That will teach you to realize that people are watching, Manny Mill. They are watching to see what kind of a guy you really are." I was a negative influence for the kingdom that time. Until then, I was not aware that people were watching me. The ministry had gained a little notoriety in the community, and with my looks and my accent, people usually remembered me. I should have exercised more self-control, just because people were watching. I didn't have to defend "my rights."

The shame of it was that I did feel so petty about a parking space. I missed God's best by making my selfish needs more important than accepting the circumstance as God's providence. Simply blessing my hasty neighbor would have pleased God and saved me a whole lot of irritation. Moreover, I never gave a thought to the possibility that he had a legitimate need to get in and out quickly and maybe God meant to use me to answer his prayer.

Another situation helped me understand that even when my motive pleased God, my method had to please Him as well. This incident involved a resident at Koinonia House, Corey Bush, who was encouraged to apply for a Colson Scholarship. Unexpectedly, the college declared a moratorium on scholarship applications, so Corey applied through the normal admissions channels and received a letter of acceptance to attend Wheaton College. We were exploring options to help Corey pay for school. In one of my meetings with Mr. Pollard, who had succeeded Ken Wessner as Chairman and CEO of Service-Master Corporation and as Chairman of the board of trustees at Wheaton College, I mentioned Corey's situation, and Mr. Pollard said he would look into the matter. A couple of days later, Corey was called in for a personal interview with a representative from the scholarship committee. He was asked to reveal detailed information about his felony conviction, which had already been appropriately disclosed in his college application. The result of this conversation was another letter in the mail, retracting his admission status, because he was considered dangerous and too much of a risk to the other students at the college.

None of this made sense to me. It was precisely because the college had a special scholarship program for Christians like Corey that we expected him to be welcomed. When I began to inquire about what happened I was told to save my persuasive influence for something more important than Corey. In my heart, there was no cause more important than that of a Christian ex-prisoner.

It seemed I must go to the top, so I made an appointment with the college president, Dr. Duane Litfin. His secretary told me that I had only five minutes. I was grateful for any minutes; however, Dr. Litfin spent over an hour with me. I was very upset. My attempt to defend Corey seemed to fail; I left weeping because I could not understand how Corey's past was any more of a risk to students than mine. Within an hour, Mr. Pollard called me on his cell phone. He wanted me to apologize to the college president. I was stubborn. "Mr. Pollard, you need to understand that I didn't do anything."

"I don't want to hear it, Manny. You need to go and apologize, now."

"Let me explain what happened."

"No. Just go back and apologize, *now.*"

"Bu . . . bu . . . bu . . . but Mr. Pollard, let me tell you just . . ."

"I don't have time to deal with it right now. You go back and apologize, and let me tell you why. In life it is very easy to make enemies. It is very difficult to make friends. And you need to be in the making friends business." End of conversation.

I called the president's office, and when the secretary answered, I said, "This is Manny Mill." Of course, she knew who I was, because I had just stormed out of the office crying.

She said, "Well, Manny, he is just about to leave for three weeks at Honey Rock to do some writing."

"Could you give him a message from me? I am calling because Mr. Bill Pollard just spoke to me, and I need to apologize to him."

"Wait, wait a moment, please." She put me on hold for a minute or so, and then Dr. Litfin picked up.

"I would like to apologize to you," I said, "and ask for your forgiveness for the way I spoke to you, and for storming out of your office because of how upset I was. Would you forgive me?"

"Oh, Manny, we all get upset. There is nothing to forgive, Manny, but yes, I forgive you. Everything is OK," he said.

"Well, I want to make sure that I regain the relationship that we had prior to this."

"Sure. Sure. We will." He was short and to

the point, but no less sincere. He was a man of his word and our relationship was restored and continued to grow stronger.

I was not wrong to defend Corey, but I was wrong in the way I treated Dr. Litfin. Humbling myself, I let go of my right to be right, and that gave the Holy Spirit far more freedom to work. The college wrestled with Corey's situation, resolved to reinstate his acceptance, and awarded him a Colson Scholarship. He completed two degrees, and I had the privilege of being present for both graduation ceremonies. Mr. Pollard gave me a "thumbs up" from where he sat up on the platform. He told me, "I'm so glad you went to bat for Corey."

About the time that Corey was leaving Koinonia House to move on campus, Eddie Wells was preparing for his release from Vienna Correctional Center. He had not been a Christian very long, and he was not all that interested in Koinonia House. Another Christian inmate named Tyrone persuaded Eddie to send us his application. We received it just before I was scheduled to speak at Vienna. Knowing that I didn't make that six-hour trip very often, I seized the opportunity. Chaplain Bill Gholson gladly arranged for me to talk with Eddie after the worship service.

"This isn't an official interview," I told Eddie. "The selection process has to be completed and we won't have enough time to do that before you get out. But I really believe that the Holy Spirit wants me to help you." I explained how he might have to live in a few different places, and that he might not ever move into the Koinonia House, but I promised to help him. I saw that Eddie wanted to be helped and that motivated me to do everything I could for him.

My plan was to have Eddie sleep at Jorge Valdes' home, but have his meals with us, attend biblical discipleship in the morning and do work projects in the afternoon, at least until the selection committee made a decision either way. My home church, First Baptist of Wheaton, was willing to sponsor him, and they had two mentors ready.

On the day Eddie was released, they also released his friend, Tyrone. I was speaking in California at the time. No one from Koinonia House was waiting at the prison gate for Eddie. One of Tyrone's friends picked him up and drove him to Carol Stream. Eddie caught a ride with them, so they dropped him off in Wheaton and he spent a few hours talking with Barbara before Jorge came by to get Eddie. They talked a lot about Eddie's ex-wife, Phyllis, which remained a source of contention between us for the first several months of his stay.

A couple of days later, to his amazement, Eddie and I were off to Atwood, Illinois, for a weeklong conference. Obtaining his travel permit from the parole office was a result of my relentless persistence, but it seemed miraculous to Eddie. He just didn't know me that well yet. When I lectured him during the whole three-hour ride about relationships with women and Phyllis in particular, he may have had second thoughts about his miraculous travel permit!

I was stressing to him the importance of "following the plan," and how he must stay focused on Christ if he was going to succeed as a Christian outside prison. Yet here I was, not "following the plan" when it came to choosing the residents. I had consulted with board members before I implemented my plan to help Eddie, and after spending so much time together at the conference, I was convinced that this modification to the normal process was the right thing to do. I was not sensitive to the fact that I put the selection committee in an awkward position. I told everyone how Eddie shared his testimony at the conference, and how God used him to bless many other people. He had already been out in public representing the ministry. Turning him down now seemed out of the question, but the selection committee was not a group of "yes people."

Pushy Manny Mill did it again, Barbara thought, but she didn't share that with me right away. She was questioning the timing of accepting

Eddie, understanding that my motive was genuine, but my method was manipulative. I still struggle with wanting to do whatever it takes to accomplish the goal. I am still learning to discern how much is my responsibility and how much should be left in God's providential hands. In other words, I have to know when I should be pushy and when I should back off.

I don't always wait on the Lord before I jump in to do my own thing. It is hard for me to be still and know that He is God (Psalm 46:10); especially when God gives me such favor and the outcomes are so positive. Eddie did the modified plan for a month before he was officially accepted as a resident. After he graduated from Koinonia House, he and Phyllis were reunited in marriage, and I had the delightful honor of participating in the ceremony. They serve as house parents at Glenwood School for Boys in St. Charles, Illinois, where they live with their three children, Emmanuel, Edward, and Elana. Eddie also became part of the national ministry team in 2002. Barbara reminded me that when she finds herself wanting to resist me in my pushiness, she thinks about Eddie, and she prays for God to show us exactly what He wants us to do.

12
·
Family
RESTORATION

NOTHING OF ETERNAL VALUE has happened in my life without prayer. God doesn't need anybody to assist Him, but in His providence, He chooses to use people to accomplish His will on earth. Without people involved in my life, without people praying for me and praying for everything that God wanted to do in my life, I would not have a God-glorifying story to tell.

FAITH OF MY FATHER

On one occasion, I was officiating at a wedding and invited my dad and my niece, Michelle, to meet me in Florida. We were at a hotel in Miami Beach, riding down the elevator from the fourteenth floor, when it stopped on the sixth floor. A man entered and said, "Hello."

"Hello," I replied and rode in silence until we reached the first floor lobby.

My dad was visibly upset and challenged me with questions. "What kind of a pastor are you that you didn't witness to that man? You don't even know if he is a Christian or not! What if he dies today and goes to hell and you didn't witness to him?"

I defended myself by saying I took a couple days off.

He said, "You don't take a vacation from being a Christian." He was determined to witness to anybody who crossed his path, and that made an impression on me. I sensed his disappointment with my apparent lack of zeal.

When we were all at Tía Nora's for dinner that night and he was witnessing to them, he kept looking up at me, expecting me to say something. Finally, I told him, "Lighten up!"

He was upset again, because I was not witnessing to the family about Jesus. He was radically committed to make sure that everyone heard about Jesus, which was encouraging for me to see. His change was for real, this man who had never believed in God's Son. He never used to believe that there was a God at all. I left Miami overjoyed that my once atheist father was now an on-fire Christian, sold out for Christ and continually feasting on God's Word. This particular experience gave me certainty and strength when I was faced with preaching at his funeral.

The funeral home in Union City was jam-packed. So many people from his neighborhood came that there was a waiting line outside. The doors were left open while we held the service. Pastor Angel Sanchez, my parents' pastor, led the service, but he asked me to give the main message. My job was to preach the Gospel clearly and to do it in a way that the people who knew my dad would understand the change in his life. I explained how he used to drink and smoke cigars, but when he got to know Jesus, he just quit. No more whiskey. No more cigars. No more cigarettes. No more cussing. Amazing! Total deliverance, after probably forty-five years of these habits. God cleaned up his language and his temper, and he became a brand-new man (2 Corinthians 5:17). The change in my dad's behavior was tremendous, and many people testified to me about that.

I came to know Jesus in my early thirties, and my dad was in his late fifties. All that time wasted, time that didn't count for anything, really, gave us an urgent purpose, a passion to glorify God. The last fifteen years of my dad's life were abundantly fruitful, and many came to know Jesus because of his bold witness for the

Lord Jesus Christ, so that was an encouraging day for me and my family.

Barbara and the boys were not with me at the funeral, because we had just been home to visit my dad a few weeks earlier. With his casket right behind me, I don't know how I made it through the service and was able to preach, except that the Holy Ghost gave me the courage and the right words. I didn't even shed a tear during that time. When I finished, Pastor Sanchez did an altar call, and God used my dad's life to bring about sixty more people into His kingdom that day.

MY SPIRITUAL FATHER'S HOMEGOING

Ken Wessner was the first person outside of prison to form a close bond with me, and when the Lord took him home, I was devastated. At his memorial service, I found myself on the platform with several godly men of influence, including Bill Pollard, Chairman and CEO of ServiceMaster Corporation, Richard Chase, President Emeritus of Wheaton College, and Chuck Colson. I felt I didn't belong, and Ken probably knew I would feel that way, so even in his death he blessed me by requesting that I speak at this service.

I was a rookie Christian and a rookie speaker at that time, and the personal loss I felt was heavy. The Holy Spirit strengthened my heart and mind so that I was able to speak without stuttering, but my usual effervescence was fizzed out. I needed to laugh, but even the timing on my jokes was off. When I began to talk about how much Ken shaped my life, my heart burned with love for Ken and love for my Jesus who brought us together. I told the story of how we met, and, finally, the joy of laughter broke through for a brief moment of relief.

Toward the end of the service, Judi and Jack Harrison, Ken's niece and nephew, sang together. Their music was irresistible to my sorrowful soul, and I could no longer contain my bereavement. I sobbed and sobbed right in front of everyone. I knew my friend was face-to-face with Jesus, but the loss I felt was too overwhelming for me to carry. Unashamed, I wept for myself, really. I had to give it all to Jesus right then and there, and ask for strength to see beyond the moment. The men sitting on either side of me patted my back as I held my head in my hands, my body shaking with grief. The Holy Spirit reminded me that He would not leave me alone, nor without earthly comfort.

A New Mentor

I knew I needed people in my life to carry on where Ken left off. In the lobby of College

Church after the service, Dick Armstrong, senior vice president of ServiceMaster Corporation, approached me to offer comfort. "Manny," he said, as he put his arm around me, "I know how much Ken meant to you. I cannot replace him in your life; however, I am promising you that I will pray for you every day as I know Ken did." He has been faithful to that promise and became a friend to me.

I walked over to Bob Cook, Norma Wessner's brother. Bob was one of the pallbearers, and they had just taken Ken's casket out of the sanctuary, preparing to go to the cemetery. I was still pretty shaken up, but I felt the Spirit prodding me to speak with Bob.

"I have lost Ken now. I need someone to take his place."

"Manny, I cannot take his place. I can't do the things for you that Ken did," Bob replied softly.

"That's not what I am talking about. I need someone that I can talk to, someone that I know is with me."

Under the circumstances, Bob could not resist my appeal. He often said he had difficulty resisting me, anyway, but we did not know each other all that well then. He must have sensed that the Lord was in it, and he answered, "Manny, I will do what I can." He lived in Springfield, Illinois, then, two hundred miles away. A few years later he and his wife, Jean, moved to Colorado Springs, a thousand miles away, but we have stayed close through telephone calls, memos, and emails.

Bob is one of the few people who have said to me, "I thank the Lord for emails." My email messages tended to be too long, too frequent, and too full of capital letters, underlining, and bold type. They were very similar to my Spanglish memos from before I learned to use email. Nevertheless, God gave me much favor with Bob, especially when I wrote too fast and left out important words like *not*. Bob has always been ready and willing to understand me and accept me just as I am.

Bob has served on the Koinonia House National Board of Trustees since its formation in 1997. The national ministry is dedicated to developing postprison ministry leaders and providing the support needed to have these leaders open more Koinonia House ministries across the nation. Bob admitted that he would never have chosen postprison ministry on his own. He says he has never seen a more difficult ministry, and he wouldn't be doing it except for me.

A CHANCE TO MENTOR OTHERS

A lot of people have told me that God used me to get them excited about ministry in general, and prisoners in particular. Hans Finzel, for example, came from a rough background in drugs and crime and many arrests, but he had never been incarcerated due to a conviction. Even a tough guy like Hans had apprehension about accompanying me to spend a Sunday afternoon in East Moline Correctional Center. He told me afterward, "Oh my goodness, I had no idea how scary prisons are! For the average Christian in the U.S., to even think of having a conversation with a convict, it is so intimidating." Yet Hans experienced the joy that comes from being willing to go into prison and be real about Jesus.

"Just to watch you operate was a tremendous blessing," Hans said. "It was huge just to see how people loved you, and respected you, and responded to you; the correctional officers and the wardens, not just Chaplain Steve Hayes and the inmates."

"They responded to the Christ in me," I told Hans. "The Holy Spirit prepared their hearts to respond. All I did was obey my Lord and go."

As intimidating as in-prison ministry might seem, I have learned over the years that post-prison ministry is much more so. Every day of my life is spent demonstrating the joy we get when we obey Christ and love our neighbors coming out of prison. Before I ever got to know him, Clarence Shuler, who later became a national board member, once had an ex-prisoner named Ernie live in his home. He was living in Tulsa, Oklahoma, at the time, the pastor of a church he had planted about three years earlier.

Clarence asked Ernie to live with them only after his wife, Brenda, said that keeping him in a motel was taking too much time away from their family. She asked Clarence, "Are you having Ernie stay in a motel because you are worried about the safety of the girls and me? Is that your only reason?"

When he said, "Yes," Brenda said, "Bring him home. We've got to practice what we are preaching!"

After Clarence moved to Colorado Springs, we were introduced through our mutual friend, Bob Cook. So naturally, when he called to tell me he would be in town, I offered him hospitality at Koinonia House.

Clarence, who is African-American, was impressed that a white guy, John Sakala, gave up his room so that Clarence could stay upstairs with the other residents. Then he thought about the situation, and he realized he was in a potentially vulnerable situation—that the others could have taken everything he owned. Forgetting the lessons he learned with Ernie, he had to challenge himself again to trust that they had been truly redeemed. He fell in love with the guys and was refreshed to see a true example of the credibility of the Gospel.

God gave me opportunities to invest in others the way so many had invested in me. One morning I received a phone call from a Wheaton professor, Dr. Walter Ellwell, who had a student in prison. Jorge Valdes was taking a correspondence course for his master's degree, and Dr. Ellwell wanted permission to have Jorge call me, thinking that we had a lot in common. We were both Cuban, both convicted felons, and brothers in the Lord Jesus Christ. Jorge needed some encouragement. He had to appear in court on a writ. He was anticipating that he would spend the rest of his life behind bars.

"Of course, he can call me. Anybody can call me." At Koinonia House, we loved to hear from Christian prisoners, and Cubans love to hear from anybody! Jorge and I began to get to know each other over the phone while he was in the Miami Metropolitan Correctional Center. Not long after that, he was released due to a legal technicality; just that quickly, Jorge was paroled to Wheaton and lived with us for two or three weeks. Now he could finish his master's degree at Wheaton College, in person rather than from prison! By God's providence, he was assigned to the same federal parole office that I had had, and his PO turned out to be my PO's partner. When I went with Jorge to check in the first time, I introduced him as my friend. A former Wheaton College student on federal parole set a precedent of full cooperation, and Jorge received favor from that, by God's grace. Because his family was still in Florida, his requests for travel permits were granted and he freely traveled back and forth.

Jorge told me that he had been one of the biggest drug dealers in the U.S., the only guy still alive from the Colombia Medellín Cartel. Everybody else had been killed. Some people thought that I was crazy to have Jorge stay at the house, that I was putting my family at risk. Barbara and I talked it over and we were not scared. We were there to love Jorge, and love conquers fear. He was not an applicant for the ministry, but he benefited from our experience in post-prison ministry. He had been locked up for eleven years, and although he had many skills that most prisoners do not have, he faced adjustments getting settled in Wheaton. Learning to live as a Christian outside prison was new for him, so Jorge called me his role model for that. He needed a friend, a mentor, and I was glad to be able to be there for him.

Jorge came over to the house often, and was a great blessing to residents of Koinonia House. That was a way that we all gave back to God, by helping others whenever we could. Jorge met his wife, Sujey, while attending graduate school, and they gave me the privilege of officiating at their wedding ceremony.

Over the years since my own graduation, I

have been asked to speak in various college classes. On one occasion, a young man named Kevin raised his hand and said, "I know who you are. I chose to attend Wheaton College because of you. My father wrote a recommendation letter for you when you were in prison, working at UNICOR. We never heard of Wheaton College before. My dad told me that one day I would go to Wheaton College."

Kevin and his father, Rick Juliano, both came to visit us at the Koinonia House. Perhaps because of his prison upbringing at Allenwood, Kevin was more comfortable with our ministry "family" than most college students were. We sure enjoyed his visits while he was at Wheaton.

LOOKING BACK, GOING FORWARD

Barbara and I were invited twice to the federal prison camp at Allenwood to do marriage seminars. The first time going back was memorable for me. Because I had a burning desire to be as *Coram Deo* as possible, especially with Barbara, I wanted her to know where I had been and where my own sin took me, to experience it somehow, so she could understand how much God had done for me. She saw Dorm Number Seven, where I lived for twenty-one months, and she met Mr. Martello, my former boss. Going back to the prison with Barbara really displayed

Christ's radically redemptive work in me. As an inmate, I attended a marriage seminar alone because my former wife had already left me. I had no clue that I would ever be married again. Now I was a free man, visiting Allenwood to lead the marriage seminar with Barbara. Whoa. What a mighty God we serve.

Every Christian receives the indwelling of the Holy Spirit at conversion, and at least one spiritual gift. I received the gift of preaching, and I learned very quickly that I had to depend on the Holy Spirit in order to exercise that gift appropriately. I hungered and thirsted for more of God's Spirit, and He never disappointed me. He also gave me the desire to do what was right in His eyes. That has been my passion since my spiritual birth. Doing what is right assumes knowing what is right, and that requires passion for God's Word. I was convinced that I must have my conscience anchored to God's truth in order to do His will in all circumstances. I wish I could say that I now do His will at all times. Though I have failed many times, I remain committed to improve daily.

The imagery of anchoring resonates with me. A boat cannot anchor in shallow water, because without depth, the water couldn't hold the boat where it needed to stay. Just the same, I could not anchor on shallow faith, because I would not have enough truth to keep me where

I needed to be. My relationship with Christ had to go deep. My knowledge of Scripture had to go deep, and intellectual knowledge alone would not anchor my conscience. Only the truth firmly deposited by the Holy Spirit in my heart affected my actions and caused me to do what was right in the eyes of the Lord.

Before Jesus found me, I was living a life that was less than shallow. I had no connection whatsoever to God; I had no interest in God; I had no care for God. My life was me, myself, and I; I served Manny Mill, and I did what I wanted. My motivation was to please myself, and all it really did was hurt me. When God delivered me, He convinced me that everything needed to change: the way I treated possessions, the way I treated my body, and especially the way I treated women. First I had to realize that women weren't possessions. Women were human beings created in the image of God. Then God put to death my inappropriate sexual desires. He did that not by taking away that love for pleasure, but by replacing it with love for a holy God, replacing it with love for a God whom I wanted to please more than I wanted to please myself. I became willing to forgo pleasure in order to please Him. God delivered me from that horrible sin of sexual addiction, gross sexual immorality. When I met my wife, Barbara, I was ready to be a Christian husband. I was able to treat her the way a woman of God should be treated, as a daughter of the King, as a person to be loved, cherished, and respected, not abused like I abused my former wife and so many other women.

I had not seen my children since they visited me in prison, and I felt like I might never see them again. Barbara and I prayed fervently, asking God to intervene. The answer to this prayer came when the DuPage County Sheriff's Department knocked on our door very early one morning. I was served papers to appear in court about child support payments. We went to court immediately and resolved the issues. I paid some child support while in prison, although it was not nearly enough.

When I appeared in court, we established child support payments. We also made payments toward the amount I was unable to pay while in prison. The judge provided my former wife's address and, after four years, I finally knew where my children lived. We had no agreement for visitation, but Barbara and I started getting to know them by telephone. In July of 1992, they came to Wheaton for a visit. Cesia was seven and Manny Jr. was twelve. When we told the children that Barbara was pregnant, Cesia was so excited; she flew up the stairs to tell the Koinonia House residents that a new baby was on the way.

Our Christian family at World Relief threw us a surprise "Children's Shower," with unique gifts like certificates to go have ice cream, money to pay for a trip to a museum, and other fun family activities. We had such a great time together that Cecilia kindly allowed them to stay an extra week. Then in late August, just as school was to begin, Hurricane Andrew hit Homestead, Florida. Cecilia and her husband lost their home and all their possessions. Thank God, they escaped alive. Faced with the challenge of rebuilding their lives, Cecilia and her husband thought it best for Manny Jr. to be able to begin school on time, and so requested that he come live with us. Although we were saddened by the devastation, we were overjoyed that God used the hurricane to give us two years with Manny Jr.

A GROWING FAMILY

Six months after Manny settled in with us, Barbara delivered our son. Named for Barbara's father and my spiritual father, Howard Kenneth Mill arrived on February 25, 1993. Manny Jr. was a huge help with his new brother. Those middle school years flew by, and Manny Jr. returned to Florida to attend high school.

Kenneth James Mill, also named after Ken Wessner and my favorite book of the Bible, arrived on October 4, 1995, with no help from me. I had surgery the day before and couldn't even drive. Barbara's parents came from Pennsylvania to help us, and when Barbara realized that she needed to get to the hospital, I could barely move to get myself dressed. Barbara told me, "Hurry up! This baby isn't going to wait for you!"

Mr. Linde heard what Barbara said, and he drove the car as if it were a carriage drawn by wild horses. Barbara had to plead with him, "Slow down, Daddy. We need to make it to the hospital alive!"

Raising two young boys in a postprison home was an adventure. I was not a good father to Manny Jr. and Cesia when they were small, and I did not want to miss out on the blessings of fatherhood with Howard and Kenneth. I was eager to handle their nighttime rituals, including baths, back scratches, and bedside prayers together. Of course, as soon as they could stand up on their own, I had them out in the yard learning to throw a baseball. Now I find myself looking forward to afternoon practices and Saturday morning baseball games. To my own surprise, I donned all the gear, went rollerblading with them, and lived to tell about it. Barbara has a photo to prove it, in case I decide to forget that I learned how to skate.

I was at a park playing with my sons when I

noticed another father with his three boys. I was
playing catch and calling out, "Throw it here,
Howud. Throw it here, *Howud!*" After a while,
Howard went over to the other boys and asked
them to build a sand castle with him. I sat down
on a bench to read my Bible. Their father cau-
tiously came toward me and said, "I'm impressed that you can find time to do devotions
when you're alone with your boys. I'm never able
to pull that off."

"You're a Christian!" I responded with excitement. He introduced himself as Gary
Reynolds and sat with me for about an hour or
so while our boys played together. We talked
about many things and ended our time by setting a date for lunch. A few days later I found
myself introducing Gary to everyone I knew, including Jorge Valdes who happened to be in
town, as my very good friend that I met by divine providence. I know, I could say the same
thing about Jorge, and it would still be true. I
wholeheartedly believe that God orchestrates
these meetings, and I do not want to miss what
He has for me by way of other people. I had a
good laugh when Gary told me how he mistook
my New Jersey, Cuban accent for a Jewish guy
from the east coast. Well, he was half-right!
Gary is just one example of the many people
God used to shape me into a godly father—not
that I have arrived, but I am committed to stay

on the road, where before I was not even on the
map.

I know I can never make up for the lost
years with Manny Jr. and Cesia, but Barbara and
I continually pray for God to show us how we
can be a blessing to them. Manny Jr. married in
May of 2000. He and his wife, Loise, blessed us
with our first grandson, Adrian. I wept openly
when I read the message Manny Jr. sent in an e-
mail, telling me he loved me and he wanted to
live his life for Christ the way he knew that I
did. In 2002, Cesia turned eighteen, and shortly
afterward moved to Wheaton to live with me
and Barbara and our sons—another tremendous
blessing from God. Barbara enjoys Cesia's female companionship and Cesia helps so much,
especially with her wonderful Cuban cooking.

Jude's son, James, also helped us, back when
we first began home-schooling. Howard was
starting first grade and Barbara agreed to home-
school James for his eighth grade year so that
Jude could devote more of her time to the ministry. Kenneth was in no particular grade yet, but
he joined in wherever the action was. That was a
special year of bonding between our three boys,
and even for me with James. He is only a year
younger than Cesia, so that gave me some more
experience with an older child, and James got a
taste of what it's like to be an older brother.
"They had a lot of energy, and I had to work really

hard to try to keep up with them," James recalled. Sounds more like a taste of fatherhood to
me!

At the end of the school year, we graduated
James during a Sunday worship service at his
church. We honored all the graduates in the
congregation, and then continued with a special
ceremony. I gave a graduation address and Barbara presented his diploma. "I'm really glad we
had the ceremony," James said recently. "You
talked about being on fire for the Lord. That was
no surprise," he laughed. "But I will always remember it," he said with a smile.

A NEW DAUGHTER

There are some events in my life that I wish
I didn't always remember, because they are
painful and humiliating. One of those times was
when my first marriage was doing so poorly that
even I noticed. I decided to leave Cecilia and
Manny Jr. and bought a second home where I
lived with another woman, Cookie. Sadly, I have
to admit that I am not clear about how long I was
gone. Nor can I honestly say exactly what caused
me to go back to Cecilia. Perhaps it was my
Cuban blood—the thought of losing my son was
intolerable. I did not know that when I broke off
my relationship with Cookie, she was already
pregnant. That was about the time Cecilia and I

decided to move to Florida, so I never saw Cookie again for the next twenty years.

Just before her nineteenth birthday, my daughter Sasha decided to find her biological father. She contacted my relatives in Union City, but never left any information on how to reach her. My family did not feel the freedom to give out my phone number, but my niece, Michelle, called and told me, "A girl who says she is your daughter is looking for you. She called me today," which happened to be September 11, 2001. Not really knowing what to do about this news, we sought counsel from a wise friend, Pastor John Bell. He advised us to pray and wait for her to come to us. We had plans to vacation in Ocean City, New Jersey, in just a few weeks. The old Manny Mill would have used his connections to find out who was looking for him. Instead, I took Pastor Bell's counsel to heart, and quietly prayed over the situation.

About a year later, Howard answered the phone in the basement, and Barbara overheard his conversation. After a few minutes of repeated, "Uh-huh. Uh-hum. Uh-huh, uh-hum," he shouted up the steps, "Mom, someone's on the phone for daddy. She says she's a relative."

I was just pulling the van into the driveway when Barbara came out the back door. "Your daughter is on the phone," she revealed. Just the way she said it let me know, but after a long pause, her words confirmed my thought. "And it's not Cesia."

I answered the call with a very guarded "Hello?"

"Is your name Manny Mill?" the voice asked. "Yes," I replied.

"Have you ever lived in Union City, New Jersey?"

"Yes, I have."

"Do you know a woman named Cookie?"

"Yes, I do." And then she began to cry. Through the tears, she said, "I believe I am your daughter."

As she continued to talk, I asked the Holy Spirit for help to be able to listen to her and be sensitive to what she was telling me. When it was my turn to speak, I immediately repented before her, asking forgiveness for my sinful behavior, committing adultery and not being married to her mother. I explained that I am now a Christian, that I already repented before God and through His Son, Jesus, I have been forgiven by God. I told her about Barbara's little saying that God never tires of new beginnings, and I wanted to have a new beginning with her. Without any excuses, I asked Sasha to forgive me for not being there for her during these last nineteen years, and asked her to give me the opportunity to earn her trust so that maybe someday she would be able to call me daddy.

Sasha told me about all the dead ends she experienced trying to track down my phone number. She was recently introduced to cyberspace, and found us on the Internet White Pages. I was pleased that she showed such courage, telephoning the very same day that she finally located our number. Just as with Manny Jr. and Cesia, we began to get to know one another over the telephone, and exchanged several pictures. When Barbara saw Sasha's photo, she said to me, "You don't need any DNA test. All she needs is a mustache!" Barbara was embarrassed when I repeated her comment to Sasha the next time she called, but Sasha replied, laughing, "That's just what my mom always says."

During the fall of 2002, we had an opportunity to be in New Jersey, and we arranged to meet Sasha face-to-face. Naturally, I was concerned about where to meet, because I desperately wanted to avoid Sasha's mother, Cookie. We met at a McDonald's in Union City, not far from my mom's home. Just before we arrived, Cookie dropped off Sasha and her children.

I was at the back of the van, looking for the gifts we brought for Sasha and her family. As Barbara stepped out of the van, Cookie was standing by her car, parked next to us. Being the only *gringa* in sight, Cookie figured that Barbara must be my wife and she said, "They're already inside."

Barbara came to the back of the van and said, "That's Cookie over there." In my heart I didn't want to see her, so I continued with my task, hoping the van would hide me. The Holy Spirit dealt with me, and later that day I had to come out of hiding.

Sasha had an old photo of her mother and me standing next to my spotless burgundy Mercedes 380SL. I wore a gold watch, a gold ring with "Manny" engraved on it, and a gold bracelet with the letters "Manny" spelled out in diamonds— vanity to the max. She had a few other pictures from my past.

"I am glad that you have saved these pictures," I spoke gently, "but I have some news to tell you. The daddy that you see there is dead." That took her by surprise. "The daddy that you see now—" I pointed to myself —"if this is who you want to get to know, he is a new creation in Jesus Christ." So that was the first gospel seed that I planted for my new daughter. Hopefully the Holy Spirit will keep it in there, and put some holy water on it so it can grow.

Sasha grew up knowing about me. "I want you to know," she volunteered, "that my mother never spoke badly about you." I was very grateful to hear that.

When we finished our visit at McDonald's, I was not ready to let her go, so I asked Sasha, "Do you want to meet my mother right now?"

She said, "Yeah!"

I called my mom and I asked, "Do you want to meet your new granddaughter and your great-grandchildren?"

She said, "Yes, bring them over."

We had a wonderful visit with my mom. When the time came for her to leave, I wanted to stay on the fifth floor with my mother, but the Holy Spirit insisted that we all go downstairs and wait with Sasha. "You are going to be a man," the Holy Spirit spoke to my heart, "and I will give you courage to do what is right in My eyes. You are going to face your daughter's mother." I thought to myself about the twenty years of damage I caused. Did I want to begin to fix it, or did I just want to put a bandage on the problem? The challenge at that moment was to let my daughter and my grandchildren see Jesus in me clearly, without any hindrance, without any fog.

After we had waited only a few minutes, Cookie and her husband drove up. God blessed my obedience, even though I had hesitated. I faced Cookie for the first time in more than twenty years. We greeted each other, and she even gave me a kiss on the cheek. She spoke to Barbara for three or four minutes, and I met her husband of fifteen years. Cookie thanked me for being there. Doing the right thing didn't feel good to me, but the flood of God's peace that washed away my fears confirmed again that Jesus would always be with me, especially in the midst of turbulent times.

I wrote a letter to Manny Jr. and Cesia, confessing my terrible sexual behavior, and introducing them to their other sister, Sasha, whom I had just met. Sasha is married to Jerry and they have twins, Justin and Alyssa. In my first draft, I said, "Since I repented of this behavior, I *have tried my best* to live my life to the glory of God." As Barbara and I reread that sentence, we realized that it left too much room for excuses. It was not strong enough just to try my best. We changed the sentence. "Since I have repented from this sinful behavior, I have *committed by God's grace not to do it again,* for the glory of God."

I wanted my children to know that yes, in my flesh I could be weak, but I was not leaving this up to my flesh. God's grace is not weak (2 Corinthians 12:9). God's Spirit is not weak. Since I was committed to keep myself anchored to His strength (Ephesians 1:19–20), He would keep me from doing it again. I truly meant that, and my children knew it. After personal conversations with both Manny Jr. and Cesia, I received their forgiveness, and they welcomed a future opportunity to meet their sister.

JESUS IS REAL

Sixteen years to the day since my salvation, on January 28, 2002, I spoke to Wheaton College students, faculty, and staff during their morning chapel service. I was privileged to be in the pulpit at my alma mater and give back to the college community that gave so much to me. The title of my message was "Jesus Is the Real Deal," and I simply told my own experience of the real Jesus and how He changed my life. I had no idea that a year later I would be writing the expanded version of that message in this book. The exciting part of the message for me was the fact that the real Jesus is the one thing I have to offer anyone. If my life and my example meant anything to anyone, then they needed to take Jesus seriously and receive the gift of life that He offered. I challenged students not to leave without knowing for sure that Jesus was real in their own life. Several of us from Koinonia House ministries stayed more than two hours after the service to pray with students who accepted that challenge.

Anyone who has known me at all would agree that my passion for God has grown stronger over the years. I committed to be a change agent for Jesus, letting my passion show, yet being sensitive to the Holy Spirit who does the changing. David Wessner, Ken's son, testified to this. He told me that through my life he can see how the Spirit moves. He can feel the Spirit's love, warmth, and passion through my life.

For some people, passion like that can be confusing and maybe even scary. Bob Cook has learned to warn people ahead of time about my passion. Too bad Bob wasn't around to warn Pastor Barry Kolb. He came to visit me at the office not long after I spoke on a Sunday to his congregation in La Fox, Illinois. He told Jude, "The guy kind of exploded out of his office, exploded all over me, and I'm not really used to being around people like that. I'm kind of quiet and laid back myself, and he is like a hand grenade that goes off on you, and he just blew me away." He was amused at first at my tendency to introduce everyone around a table as "my good friend so-and-so," but he came to realize I meant it.

The old me manipulated people to accomplish my own gain. The new me in Christ strives to love people as He does. Those old manipulative techniques still get me in hot water sometimes, but I can honestly say that my motivation has been transformed. I labor for the King and His glory, and I still gain—I gain loads of joy! I have said many times that I am a rookie Christian. I have so much yet to learn, so much yet to do for Jesus. This is not the end of the story; it is really just the beginning.

Koinonia House National Ministries is praying and preparing for a breakthrough in postprison ministry, especially in leadership development. Chuck Colson joked about having one hundred Manny Mills, but that's not what we need. We need hundreds of postprison ministry leaders who are equipped, trained, and empowered to love our neighbors coming out of prison. I long to see the time when every day there is someone waiting by a prison gate somewhere in our country, arms open wide ready to receive a brother or sister and bring that person home to their family in Christ. I want to live long enough to see that time come. When Jesus does finally call me to my eternal home, my heart's desire will be to hear Him say those words, "Well done, good and faithful servant."

Manny's family visits him in Allenwood Federal Prison Camp. Left to right: Mom, Norma; sister, Normita; Manny; and Dad, Manolo.

At the Washington Hilton after the Washington Discipleship Seminar in 1988, with fellow inmates and their chaperone, Bob Brantley (far left), Charles Colson (third from left), Billy Graham (sixth from left). Manny is in the white suit.

·

Timeline of
MANNY
MILL'S LIFE

CHAPTER 1 – LIFE IN CUBA

1925　Manolo Mill Hernandez is born
1926　Tío René is born
1929　Norma Martinez Ochoa is born
1947　Tío René gets cursed (chapter 4)
1949　Manny's parents, Manolo and Norma,
　　　　are married
1950　Tío René is hospitalized (chapter 4)
1956　Manny is born
1959　Castro takes over Cuba
1960　Normita is born
1962　Manny begins studying judo

CHAPTER 2 – NARROW ESCAPES

1970　Mills leave Cuba and go to Spain
1972　Mills leave Spain for the U.S.

CHAPTER 3 – THE AMERICAN DREAM

1974   Manny begins producing Cuban dances
1975   Manny graduates from Union Hill High
        School – begins attending Seton Hall
        University
1976   Manny's mom becomes a Christian
        (chapter 4)
1977   Manny starts working for Union City
1979   Manny and Cecilia are married
1980   Manny Jr. is born

CHAPTER 4 – SALVATION AND FIRE

1981   Tío René becomes a Christian

CHAPTER 5 – RADICAL REDEMPTION

1982   Manny and Cecilia move to Florida
1982   Sasha is born (chapter 12)
1984   Manny commits crimes
1984   Manny and family flee to Venezuela
1984   Cesia is born
1986   (Jan) Manny and his father become
        Christians

CHAPTER 6 – COMPLICATED CONSEQUENCES

1986   (Feb) Manny and family return to the
        U.S.
1986   (July) Manny goes to prison – Allen-
        wood Federal Prison Camp
1987   Cecilia moves away and files for divorce

CHAPTER 7 – EXTRAORDINARY DISCIPLESHIP

1988   (Feb) Manny goes to Washington Discipleship Seminar, meets Ken Wessner

1988   (Apr) Manny is released from prison

CHAPTER 8 – FEDERAL PAROLE

1988   (July) Manny starts school at Wheaton College

CHAPTER 9 – BARBARA LINDE MILL

1989   Manny goes to Holy Lands and meets Barbara

CHAPTER 10 – COURTSHIP AND MARRIAGE

1990   Manny and Barbara are married

1990   Manny graduates Wheaton College –B.A. (chapter 7)

1990   Koinonia House is formed (chapter 11)

1991   Manny graduates Wheaton College –M.A.

1991   Manny is ordained

CHAPTER 11 – POSTPRISON MINISTRY

1992   (Feb) Manny and Barbara move into Koinonia House

1992   (July) Manny Jr. and Cesia come to visit in Wheaton (chapter 12)

1992   (Aug) Hurricane Andrew hits; Manny Jr. moves to Wheaton (chapter 12)

1993   Howard Kenneth Mill is born
1994   Ken Wessner dies
1995   Kenneth James Mill is born

CHAPTER 12 – FAMILY RESTORATION
1999   Koinonia House National Ministries is
        launched
2000   (Apr) Manny's father dies
2000   (May) Manny Jr. and Loise are married
2002   Manny and Barbara meet Sasha
2003   Cesia moves to Wheaton

•

Afterword

I WANT YOU TO KNOW that Manny Mill is not a larger-than-life guy. Maybe now that you've read the real story of Manny Mill, you actually think a lot less of him. I don't know. Either way is OK, because you don't need to think too much about him. You need to think about the One who changed him, Jesus Christ. He is real, and He is larger-than-life when it comes to caring for people. He really changed Manny, He changed me, and He can change anybody. We are talking about *radical* change, forever change, glorious and joyful change. Jesus is the One you need to look at. He is the reason we wrote this book, so everyone who reads it will know that God is *the* God of the universe and Jesus is His Son, in whom God is well pleased.

There is no way to be changed without Christ. Any other kind of change is temporary, because life on this earth is temporary, and those changes will die when our flesh dies. Spirit life is eternal, and our home in eternity is permanent. All of us will one day face God our Creator, Christ our Savior, and the Holy Spirit, our revealer of Truth. No one will escape that day. And when God asks you on what basis you think you should live forever with Him, there is only one answer that works: by the blood of Christ and His righteousness alone. All of us *will* live eternally, but not all of us will live eternally with Jesus. Only those who responded to His love while on earth. Only those who repented (turned away from sin and turned toward Christ) and received His forgiveness while on earth. Only Christ's sacrificial love can change hearts and produce faith.

Faith is hope in what we cannot see while on earth. After death, we will all see the truth, but that sight will no longer be faith. It will be too late to have faith in Christ. We will know the truth, we will see the truth, but the truth will no longer save those who refused to see with eyes of faith. That is the burden that every Christian living on earth carries. When the truth is revealed and no one remains deceived, it won't matter that we are "right" and those who rejected Christ are "wrong." There will be no satisfaction in saying, "I told you so." It is not about being *right*. It is about being forever with the Lord and living in the light of His love. Can't you see why Christians are so obnoxious sometimes about sharing their faith? Because they *know* the end of the story, and there is nothing they can do except plead with the Holy Spirit to show unbelievers the way to have faith now.

If you are reading this book, and you do not have faith in the Lord Jesus Christ, I beg you to consider the experiences of this man, and how Jesus Christ, Moshiach Y'shua, changed his life. Jesus is the Way, the Truth, and the Life. No one comes to the Father but by Him (John 14:6). God promised that if you sincerely seek to know the truth about Him, you will find it— you will find *Him*. Please don't wait another day.

> Because of Christ's love, I so want to be your sister in Christ,
> Jude Skallerup

Koinonia House National Ministries
P.O. Box 1415
Wheaton, IL 60189-1415
www.koinoniahouse.org

JUDE SKALLERUP is Program Director for Koinonia House® National Ministries, Inc. Her story was told on *Unshackled,* the radio ministry of Pacific Garden Mission, broadcast over 1,500 stations in 147 countries. Jude first met Manny Mill in May of 1988. Jude resides in Wheaton with her husband, Bob, son James, and Papa Jim Skallerup.

•

Acknowledgments

I f you know Manny at all, then you can imagine the list of people he truly wanted to acknowledge here. All of you should know who
you are, because we have thanked you many
times, and will continue to do so as our relationships grow. Without you, we would have no story
to tell.

God gave us an extraordinarily gifted visual
arts team that we joyfully acknowledge: Jim
and Mary Whitmer, photographers; Chuck
Haas, cover design; and Gabriel Weckesser, for
digital production of Manny's photo albums.
Thank you Valerie Merrill, Diana Longenecker,
and Nancy Niemeyer, assistants to Chuck Colson; and of course, we are grateful to Chuck for
writing the foreword.

With gratitude, we acknowledge Linda Nelson and the many people she mobilized to pray faithfully for this project. To all of you who prayed, we know our heavenly Father delighted to bless us because of your fervency. We were strengthened and supported via phone and email prayers from Norma Mill, Joyce and Howard Linde, Bud and Betty Knoedler, Manny's pastor Mike Rowe, Mark Dillon, James Lukose, John Nawrocki, Bruce Renfroe, John Sakala, Sean and Susie Salins, Jeff and Jackie Mattson, Kager and Donna Gordon, Charlie and Michele Blanck, the Jepsen family, Jeff and Claudia Barrett, Don and Mary Andre, Grace Bible Fellowship, and Faith Bible Fellowship. We thank God for our Board of Trustees who approved this project, consistently prayed, and encouraged us so often, particularly the Executive Committee: Brad Sampson, Don Whittaker, Bill France, and John Ochodnicky.

Thank you, National Writing Committee, especially Mike Hughes and Zondra Lindblade who, by your influence over the years, empowered Jude to accept the challenge and write this book. Thank you to all of you whose names appear in this story. By God's grace you are a part of who Manny Mill has become in Jesus. To those who were asked to answer all Jude's questions, thank you for finding the time it took. Thank you for being risk takers by committing to tell the truth into a tape recorder! God bless our national ministry team of Phil Foust, Jim Knoedler, Max Nieves, Dave Roberts, Gabriel Weckesser, and Eddie Wells for your faithfulness to pray daily. Dear brothers, we are humbled by your capacity to step to the plate and carry the load we left in order to dedicate ourselves to this task. The end results, including all the deadlines we met, bear witness to the *koinonia* way God has molded us to function as a team. With deep affection, we recognize our other team members, discipleship and resident directors: Mike and Vickie Covarrubias, John and Kathy Graham, and Tyrone and Roseanne Townsend, you are a testimony of God's grace by your perseverance and acceptance of this providential priority.

Many people at Moody Broadcasting and Moody Publishers have gone above and beyond to support this project. Thank you to Mark Elfstrand—you started it all; Bob Neff who opened the doors, Larry Mercer who believed in us, Greg Thornton who suggested this story, Cheryl Dunlop, our ingenious editor, Pam Pugh, our proofreader, Dave DeWit who made the production wheels roll, Amy Peterson, our author relations manager, and Karen Waddles, our human glue and detail specialist. God will reward you, Moody team, for your patience with our email messages! God bless you, Chaplain Manny

Rojas, for your patience and ability to translate Norma Mill's recorded interview during the Harvest of Hope book packing party! Norma Wessner, David and Patti Wessner, Ross and Barbie (Wessner) Anderson, thank you for your loving support and for taking time to help Jude get to know Ken. Thank you, Doreen Fast, for all the ways you are the hands and feet of Christ to Jude and her family.

No one knows better than our families what a project like this does to home life. To Barbara Mill, thank you for your faith and trust in God and for your willingness to be so transparent in this book. To Bob Skallerup, thank you for your unconditional love and your steadfast confidence in Jesus. The precious friendship among us is a gift from God, and to Him we say ¡Aleluya! To Manny Jr. and Loise, Cesia, Howard and Kenneth Mill, Sasha Greaves, and James and Papa Jim Skallerup, may the Lord bless you for all your willing sacrifices, cheerfully offered to make this book become a reality.

MANNY MILL AND JUDE SKALLERUP

About the
AUTHOR

MANNY MILL (M.A., Wheaton College Graduate School) is Executive Director of Koinonia House® National Ministries. Since 1999, Manny has been developing a core of postprison ministry leaders to equip the church to meet the needs of Christian ex-prisoners returning to society. He currently invests much of his time traveling to different churches, prisons, ministries, colleges, and conferences to present the mission to "equip, assist and support" members of the local church in their ability to embrace Christians coming out of prison. Manny has shared his story on numerous radio and television programs. He resides in Wheaton, Illinois, with his wife, Barbara.